CULTURE SMART!

# SINGAPORE

Angela Milligan and Tricia Voute

·K·U·P·E·R·A·R·D·

ISBN 978 1 85733 887 4

British Library Cataloguing in Publication Data
A CIP catalogue entry for this book is available from the British Library

First published in Great Britain
by Kuperard, an imprint of Bravo Ltd
59 Hutton Grove, London N12 8DS
Tel: +44 (0) 20 8446 2440   Fax: +44 (0) 20 8446 2441
www.culturesmart.co.uk
Inquiries: sales@kuperard.co.uk

Series Editor Geoffrey Chesler
Design Bobby Birchall

Printed in India

# About the Author

ANGELA MILLIGAN prepares individuals and families from Europe and North America for expatriate life, an important aspect of which is cultural-awareness training. She has worked in East Asia, Australia, Belgium, and Argentina, and has briefed international companies on Singapore. Her publications include *How to Survive in Style*, a practical guide for newly arrived expatriates to Britain, and *Customs and Etiquette of Australia*. Angela is a graduate in History from the University of East Anglia and a fellow of the Royal Society of Arts.

TRICIA VOUTE has a B.A. in Anthropology from Durham University and an M.A. in the Philosophy of Religion from King's College, London. She has taught philosophy in different parts of the world and written textbooks on the subject, as well as articles on cultural and faith issues in the *Times* and other publications. Tricia lived in Singapore for five years, teaching religion and philosophy at the Tanglin School. She was involved in teacher training in local schools and has Singaporean friends across the social and religious spectrum.

The Culture Smart! series is continuing to expand. All Culture Smart! guides are available as e-books, and many as audio books. For the latest titles visit

**www.culturesmart.co.uk**

The publishers would like to thank **CultureSmart!**Consulting for its help in researching and developing the concept for this series.

**CultureSmart!**Consulting creates tailor-made seminars and consultancy programs to meet a wide range of corporate, public-sector, and individual needs. Whether delivering courses on multicultural team building in the USA, preparing Chinese engineers for a posting in Europe, training call-center staff in India, or raising the awareness of police forces to the needs of diverse ethnic communities, it provides essential, practical, and powerful skills worldwide to an increasingly international workforce.

For details, visit www.culturesmartconsulting.com

**CultureSmart!**Consulting and **CultureSmart!** guides have both contributed to and featured regularly in the weekly travel program "Fast Track" on BBC World TV.

# contents

| | |
|---|---|
| Map of Singapore | 7 |
| Introduction | 8 |
| Key Facts | 10 |

**Chapter 1: LAND AND PEOPLE** — 12
* Climate — 13
* Flora and Fauna — 13
* The People — 15
* Singapore: A Brief History — 22
* Lee Kuan Yew — 32
* Social Change — 33
* Law and Order — 37
* Political Life — 38
* Urban Development — 40

**Chapter 2: VALUES AND ATTITUDES** — 42
* Common Asian Values — 42
* Religion — 43
* Education — 59
* A Goal-Driven Society — 59

**Chapter 3: CUSTOMS AND TRADITIONS** — 60
* Festivals and Holidays — 60
* The Chinese Lunar Calendar — 69
* Births — 70
* Weddings — 71
* Funerals — 76
* Gift Giving — 78

**Chapter 4: THE SINGAPOREANS AT HOME** — 82
* Social and Family Relationships — 82
* Children — 83
* Lifestyle and Housing — 84
* Invitations Home — 85

- Greetings      87
- Public Display      88
- Boy Meets Girl      89
- National Service      90
- Names      90

**Chapter 5: FOOD AND DRINK**      **94**
- Cooking Styles      94
- Dietary Restrictions      98
- Food Courts      100
- *Kopitiams*      101
- *Cze Chas*      102
- Drink      102
- Banquets and Entertaining      104

**Chapter 6: TIME OUT**      **110**
- Tourism      110
- Destinations      110
- Money      122
- Shopping      123
- Nightlife      125
- Culture      126

**Chapter 7: TRAVEL, HEALTH, AND SAFETY**      **128**
- Getting Around      128
- Where To Stay      132
- Health      133
- Rules and Regulations      136
- Safety      137

**Chapter 8: BUSINESS BRIEFING**      **140**
- The Economic Miracle      140
- Financial Management      142
- Building Relationships      143

# contents

- Introductions ..... 144
- Small Talk ..... 145
- Hands ..... 145
- Business Cards ..... 146
- Meetings ..... 146
- Women in Business ..... 147
- Saving Face ..... 148
- Negotiating Styles ..... 148
- Decision Making ..... 150
- Contracts and Fulfillment ..... 150
- Team Building ..... 151

**Chapter 9: COMMUNICATING** ..... 152
- Languages ..... 152
- Body Language ..... 158
- Humor ..... 160
- The Media ..... 160
- Telecommunications ..... 162
- The Internet ..... 162
- Postal Services ..... 163
- Conclusion ..... 164

**Further Reading** ..... 165
**Index** ..... 166

# Map of Singapore

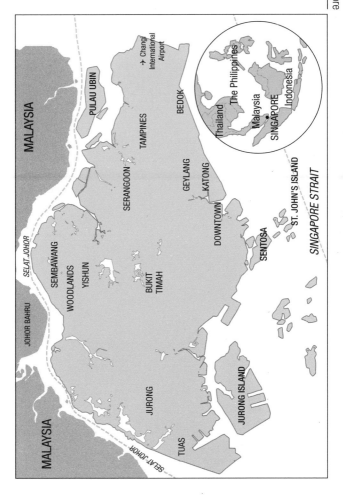

# introduction

The small island state of Singapore is unique
in the region. Not only is it a young country—
independence came in 1965—but it is a land of
immigrants, in which people from three distinct
backgrounds, Chinese, Malay, and Indian, live side
by side in harmony.

This multicultural harmony is no accident. It has
been consciously engineered by the government to
ensure the racial riots of 1964 are never repeated.
Through housing projects, Racial Harmony Day
(July 21), and free education for all, social awareness
and national pride are propagated. This is a positive,
energetic, "can do" society, whose citizens are often
worried about not keeping up with the Joneses, or,
as it is portrayed in Singapore, "*kiasu*," from the
Hokkien word meaning "to miss out."

On August 9, 1965, the national leader Lee
Kuan Yew faced the unknown when he announced
that Singapore had been forced to leave the newly
formed Federation of Malaysia. Many commentators
feared the worst; this newly created republic had
no natural resources, was tiny compared to its
neighbors, and only had its deep water harbor, its
commercial skills, and its close proximity to the rest
of Asia to rely on. Within fifteen years, however,
Singapore had transformed itself into an economic
powerhouse and become a byword for technical
excellence. Popularly known as the Little Red Dot, it
is considered the twentieth century's most successful

development story and exerts an influence on the international stage that far exceeds its size.

Yet despite Singapore's Western veneer and expat population, the visitor is quickly reminded that the "Lion City" is most definitely Asian. Although many of the traditional cultural values of the communities living there have been challenged by the demands of the modern Singaporean state, their underlying philosophies remain intact. It is therefore difficult to talk about a typical Singaporean, for this would depend on whether one were referring to someone of Chinese, Malay, or Indian descent. By and large, however, this is a goal-oriented, meritocratic society. It is also fair to say that the three ethnic groups share certain Asian values in common—belief in ordered relationships, obligation, respect for traditions, polite behavior, and the protection of face, both for oneself and for others.

*Culture Smart! Singapore* introduces the Western visitor to the rich and varied cultures and customs of Singapore's communities. It shows what motivates people, how they interact with each other and with outsiders, and tells you what to expect and how to behave in unfamiliar situations. It will also draw attention to the rapid social changes that have occurred as a result of globalization. In doing so, it offers you a fuller, more rounded experience of this fascinating society.

## Key Facts

| | | |
|---|---|---|
| **Official Name** | Republic of Singapore | Singapore is a member of ASEAN. |
| **Capital** | Singapore City | On the southeast coast of the island |
| **Area** | 279 sq miles (722 sq km) | Population density 8,000 per sq km |
| **Currency** | Singapore Dollar | |
| **Climate** | Tropical, hot 73°–90°F (23°–32°C), humid and rainy all year | There is a monsoon season from November to January. |
| **Population** | 2018: 5.6 million; 29% nonresident | |
| **Ethnic Makeup** | Chinese 76% Malay 15% Indian 7% Other 2% | |
| **Religion** | Buddhism, Taoism, Islam, Hinduism, Sikhism, Christianity, Judaism | Freedom of religion is enshrined in the Constitution. |
| **Official Languages** | Chinese (Mandarin), Malay, Tamil, English | Malay is the national language. English is the language of administration and business. |
| **Government** | Parliamentary republic, ruled by the People's Action Party since independence. The president is the head of state; the head of government is the prime minister. | The cabinet is appointed by the prime minister and is responsible to parliament. The president is elected by popular vote for six years. Elections to the unicameral parliament are held every five years. |

| | | |
|---|---|---|
| **Adult Literacy** | 99% male, 95% female | Literacy in 2 or more languages 73% |
| **Family Makeup** | Average number of children per family: 2. Infant mortality rate: 2.2 per 1,000 births | Age structure: 0–14 yrs 15%; 15–64 yrs 71%; 65 yrs + 14%. Median age: 41 yrs. Overall pop. growth: citizens 0.1% in 2017; non-resident fell 1.6%. Life expectancy: 81 yrs male, 85 yrs female |
| **Economy** | Most prosperous in Asia in terms of per capita GDP. Much of the economy is based on importing and reexporting and financial services. | Exports: electronics, manufactures, and chemicals. GDP growth rate in 2017 was 3.5%, slowing in the last quarter. |
| **Media** | Both local and international newspapers and television channels are available. | Restrictions sometimes apply where international newspapers and magazines are highly critical of the government or its policies. |
| **Electricity** | 220–240 volts, 50 Hz | |
| **Internet Domain** | .sg | |
| **Telephone** | Singapore's country code is 65. | |
| **Time Difference** | UTC/GMT + 8 hours | |

# chapter one

# LAND &
# PEOPLE

Singapore is a small island state at the southern end of the Malay Peninsula. Separated by narrow straits from mainland Malaysia, and by the Straits of Malacca from Sumatra, one of the largest islands in the Indonesian archipelago, it is approximately 31 miles (52 km) long east–west and 17 miles (27 km) wide north–south. It consists of sixty-three islands and has a population of 5.6 million people.

Singapore City, on the southeast coast of the island, marries colonial architecture with futuristic buildings and skyscrapers, some taller than the island's highest point, Bukit Timah Hill. These

buildings contain smart offices, five-star hotels, and glamorous shops. Yet despite the predominance of buildings, great thought and effort have gone into keeping the city green. The drive into the city from the airport is lined with colorful bougainvilleas and frangipani as well as travelers' palms and jacarandas, and on reclaimed land at the edge of the city is the newly created Gardens by the Bay, the country's latest botanical garden, 101 hectares in size.

## CLIMATE

The climate is tropical. Situated just 5° north of the equator, Singapore is either hot and sticky or very hot and sticky all year round. The monsoon weather, which lasts from November to January, brings heavy rain and occasional flooding, and lowers the temperature from 86°F (30°C) to 73°F (23°C). The hottest and most humid months are from March to July—but expect dramatic thunderstorms at any time of the year, usually in the afternoon. Be warned, though: many visitors catch cold, owing to the contrast of the outside temperature with the aggressive air-conditioning in the hotels and upmarket restaurants.

## FLORA AND FAUNA

Singapore's national flower is the purple and white orchid "Vanda Miss Joaquim," a natural hybrid discovered in the garden of the lady of that name and subsequently presented to the Botanical Gardens. You will see the national emblem everywhere, from tourist trinkets and politicians' shirts to the carefully packed bunches on sale at the airport. For those interested in horticulture, the National Orchid Garden merits a visit. The main attraction of the Singapore Botanic Gardens, it has a collection of 1,000 species and 2,000 hybrids. On an undulating three-hectare site, near Orchard Road, the Botanic Gardens is the oldest public park in Singapore and the country's first UNESCO Heritage site. Established in 1859, it is famous for being the birthplace of the region's rubber industry.

The new Gardens by the Bay opened in 2011 as a showpiece of garden artistry, with over one million plants and the famous Supertrees that glow Peranakan colors at night and around which there is an aerial walkway. Here you will also find the Heritage Gardens, the Canyon, and the large glass domes, one of which (the Cloud Forest) has the world's tallest indoor waterfall.

Bukit Timah Hill is the island's highest point and its last remaining pocket of primary rain forest. Many visitors stroll to the peak to see the macaque monkeys; this is best done either in the cool of the early morning or in the evening, avoiding the hottest times of the day.

Similarly, the best time to visit the Sungei Buloh Wetland Reserve on the north coast is in the early morning. This protected wetland nature park of more than 202 hectares has trails through forests, ponds, mudflats, and mangrove swamps where you can discover native species such as mudskippers, water snakes, monitor lizards, and otters. During the migratory season (from September to March) you can watch flocks of shorebirds and waders from strategically located hides.

Lastly, there is the MacRitchie Reservoir in the heart of Singapore. Built in 1867 by the philanthropist Tan Kim Seng, it is one of four reservoirs in the nature reserve and is popular with runners and water-sport enthusiasts. Along its 6.8 mile (11 km) trail, much of it through tropical rainforest, you can find long-tailed macaque monkeys, monitor lizards, and, on the odd occasion, a colugo (or flying lemur). It is also famous for the Treetop Walk, a free-standing suspension bridge that spans the reserve's two highest points.

## THE PEOPLE

Singapore is a land of immigrants. Apart from small coastal communities, it was virtually uninhabited until the nineteenth century, when Britain turned it into a strategic naval and commercial staging post, triggering substantial immigration, particularly from China. More of a salad bowl than a melting pot, the resulting society is a model of multicultural harmony. Although the Chinese are by far the largest ethnic group, the Malays who make up 15 percent of the population, and the Indians who form 7 percent, contribute more to Singaporean society than their numbers would suggest.

The official languages of Singapore are therefore Malay (which is also the "national" language), Chinese (Mandarin), Tamil, and English. English is the language of administration, business, and technology.

**The Chinese Immigrants**
During the last days of the Qing dynasty in the nineteenth century, life in China was harsh and oppressive for many. Poverty was widespread and those in the coastal provinces needed little incentive to leave. The first junk bound for Singapore sailed from Amoy in 1821, and by 1827 the local Malay population was vastly outnumbered. The British encouraged this immigration as the Chinese were considered a hardy and industrious people. Many were illiterate and penniless, but once they had paid off their passage they flourished. Some came as indentured laborers to work in the tin mines of Malaya and the docks in Singapore. They became coolies, farmers, and traders.

Their numbers grew, despite the monthly quotas imposed during the Great Depression. The administration was anxious to avoid overcrowding and unemployment, and to control the prostitution that had been a problem in the early years of the nineteenth century when most of the immigrants were young men. In the early years of the twentieth century the problem still existed, with around 240 men to every 100 women.

Today, most Chinese Singaporeans can trace their ancestry to the southern coastal provinces between Hong Kong and Shanghai, that is, from four river deltas: the Min River that flows into the South China Sea at Fuzhou, the Chiu-lung at Xiamen (Amoy), the Han River near Shantou (Swatow), and the Pearl River south of Guangzhou (Canton) and opposite Hong Kong.

Although they are all Chinese and share the same written language, they come from different ethnic groups, speak their own dialects, and have their own local cultures. The people from Fuzhou speak Hokchiu; those from Xiamen speak Hokkien (this is the largest ethnic group in Singapore); those from Shantou speak Hoklo (but are called Teochew); and those from the Pearl River delta and Guangzhou call themselves and speak Cantonese. In the early days this led to factionalism and clan conflicts in Singapore.

The Hakka, who speak Hakka, emigrated from Guangdong, Fujian, and Jianxi provinces, and the Hainanese from Hainan Island, the most southerly part of China that is opposite the Vietnamese coast.

In Singapore today, members of the older generation still speak their native dialects, but increasing numbers of young Chinese Singaporeans speak Mandarin at home.

## Straits Chinese

A group of Chinese arrived in Singapore who were
descendants of the old Chinese families of sixteenth-
century Malacca and Penang. These Straits Chinese,
or Peranakans, had intermarried with and been
influenced by their Malay neighbors. The women
adopted Malay-style dress and were referred to
as Nonya. Their cuisine adopted typical Malay
ingredients such as fragrant roots, herbs, chilies,
and, above all, coconut milk. They combined the
traditional love of pork—forbidden, of course, to
Malay Muslims—with classic Malay ingredients.

The Straits Chinese were educated, had money,
and soon found themselves an indispensable part of
the colonial administration. Some became doctors,
lawyers, and teachers, while others established
successful businesses, especially in the timber and
rubber trades. The men, referred to as the Baba
community, were often ridiculed for being "more
British than the British." Their newspapers were in
English rather than Chinese, and they adopted the
manners of their colonial masters, playing billiards
and drinking brandy. Although they did not mix
socially with the new Chinese immigrants, they
kept abreast of developments on the mainland,
especially those concerning the reform of Imperial
China's archaic system of government. It comes as
no surprise that it was a Straits Chinese, Teo Eng
Hock, who offered his large villa to Sun Yat Sen,
the future first president of China, when he sought
refuge in Singapore. To commemorate Sun Yat Sen
and his revolutionary nationalist movement, the
Singapore government restored the villa in 1964;

you can visit it from 10:00 a.m. to 5:00 p.m. and view its collection of artifacts and photographs. Nor should it surprise the reader that Lee Kuan Yew, the founding father of modern Singapore, was of Hakka and Peranakan descent (although he did not advertise the fact). An exhibition in 2015 honored fifty influential Peranakans who helped shape the country, including Tan Tock Seng the philanthropist and Chua Seng Kim, the founding president of the Singapore Woman's Association.

## The Malay Community

The original Malay inhabitants of the island were soon outnumbered by the thousands of Chinese immigrants in search of a better life. It is a testament to the strength of their community that it both survived and influenced the developing nation, with Malay becoming the national language of Singapore. In the constitution, the government recognizes the special position of the Malays as the island's indigenous people.

Gentle and courteous, their core values are generosity and hospitality. With a strong sense of community, they are also self-reliant and have prospered in the new Singapore, with Halimah Jacob, becoming president of Singapore in 2017. They do not believe in the pursuit of wealth for its own sake, but in the greater importance of the spiritual side of life. This is reflected in their concern not only for their families but for their neighbors as well.

The Malays wish visitors to enjoy Singapore and their unique culture. However, there are a few "dos and don'ts" that the visitor should be aware of and which will avoid upsetting or embarrassing your hosts. These are discussed on pages 85–7 and 144–48.

### The Indian Community

Despite making up just over 7 percent of the population, Singaporean Indians are religiously, linguistically, and economically diverse, although 60 percent are of Tamil ancestry. Known for their entrepreneurial gifts, they have also been prominent in education, politics, diplomacy, and the law.

To appreciate the culinary richness of their community and their colorful wares, it is worth visiting "Little India" on Serangoon Road including the Mustafa Centre and Tekka Market. Most Indians still shop there, especially when buying saris, men's dhotis, betel nuts, heavy brass stands, garlands for weddings, arm bangles, and other indispensable items for an Indian household.

Indian shopkeepers appreciate a customer who will haggle. If you are the first customer of the day, you can be assured of a bargain as they regard the opening purchase, however small, to be a good omen, especially if that purchase includes flowers, sugar, or sweets—but not oil. The latter is regarded as a bad sign for the rest of the day's trading.

## The Expat and Migrant Community

Immigration has not ended in Singapore and it remains essential to the country's economic growth. Non-Singaporeans are found in every area of commercial, medical, and educational life. In 2017, there were 1.4 million foreigners employed in the country of whom nearly 800,000 were domestic workers.

In 2013 the Population White Paper projected that by 2030 Singapore's population would be about 6.5 million, of which 4.2 million would be resident and 2.3 million would be non-resident. It called for an increase in the number of foreign workers, arguing that a balance needed to be maintained between the skilled and less-skilled and those who worked in domestic service. Although the paper was passed, concerns were voiced about the pressure on facilities and social cohesion. Four thousand people protested at People's Corner in Hong Lim Park and as a consequence a more cautious approach has been adopted.

A person can become a Singapore citizen through birth or via descent. It is also possible to gain citizenship through registration (naturalization) if you have been a Permanent Resident (PR) for at least two years and are employed by a registered company (which does not have to be Singaporean) or are married to a Singapore citizen. In 2017 there were 525,000 PRs in the country.

## SINGAPORE: A BRIEF HISTORY

Despite being only recently created a nation-state, Singapore has a long history, owing to its strategic position at the junction of numerous shipping routes.

### Early Days

One of the first references to Singapore is in the writings of General Lu Tai in 203 CE, who tells of an expedition sent by the Chinese Emperor to Pu-Luo-Chung, as Singapore was then known. Marco Polo may have also referred to the island when writing of the noble city of Chiamassie. Certainly, it was called Temasek by the fourteenth century and later gained the name Singapura ("Lion City" in Sanskrit) when, according to Malay legend, a Sumatran prince saw a lion there and founded a town. Favored as a port for traders taking wares from Arabia, India, and the Malay Peninsula to East and Southeast Asia and back again on the seasonal monsoon winds, it came under the influence of different Indian and Siamese kingdoms. A pawn in their internecine wars, the settlement was burned in 1613 by Portuguese raiders, after which it went into decline with traders moving to Malacca, a more fortified and secure port. Nominally under the southern Malay Sultanate of Johor, only a few people—known as sea people—remained, surviving on fishing and piracy.

The Merlion, the official mascot of Singapore, has a fish's body and a lion's head, symbolizing the country's origin as a fishing village and commemorating the legend of the lion's sighting. There are five statues, and the oldest is located at the Merlion Park at the mouth of the Singapore River.

## Colonization

In the eighteenth century, the British and the Dutch were commercial competitors in the East–West trade, while Britain and France were military enemies and sought to extend their empires in the region. By 1815 the French were defeated in Europe and no longer posed a threat to British and Dutch interests in Asia. The British and the Dutch then set out to acquire exclusive trading posts through agreements with local rulers.

Britain was represented in the region by the powerful East India Company, whose commercial strength was backed by its own military force. It sought a halfway house between Bengal, its power base, and Canton, the source of its new wealth in tea and the destination for its Indian-produced opium in which it had a monopoly. The Dutch were snapping up the best ports, and Thomas Raffles (later Sir Stamford Raffles) of the Company had long wanted to establish a trading post in the region.

"Our object is not territory but trade," he wrote, "a great commercial emporium and a fulcrum whence we may extend our influence politically as circumstances may hereafter require." He negotiated a treaty with Sultan Hussein of Johor giving Britain the right to establish a trading post on the island of Singapore and proclaim it a free port, and on February 6, 1819, the Union flag of Great Britain was officially raised. Security and stability soon attracted ships in search of a safe haven where they could repair their vessels and restock with food and water. Success was guaranteed.

Raffles was one of a special breed of freewheeling and adventurous spirits produced by Britain's great commercial empire. However else one views it today, the Empire gave scope and opportunity to British men of humble birth, many of whom became efficient and fair administrators, humanitarian in their outlook and practical in their approach.

**Raffles (1781–1826)**
Thomas Stamford Raffles was born on a slave ship (his father was the captain) in the mid-Atlantic. He was forced to leave school at the age of fourteen when his father could no longer afford the fees, but was fortunate enough to obtain a clerical position in

the East India Company in 1805. Ten years later he was on his way to Penang in northwestern Malaya to take up a position as Assistant Secretary in the government. Raffles was ambitious and he used his time on the voyage to learn Malay. He was soon considered fluent, and by 1811 he was appointed Governor of Java. After a spell back in England and a second marriage (his first wife, Olivia, having died in 1814), he was appointed Governor of Sumatra. In 1818 he persuaded the Governor General of India, Lord Hastings, to agree to an expedition to set up a trading post at the southern tip of Malacca.

Although his name is forever linked with Singapore, Raffles (he dropped the "Thomas" when knighted by the Prince Regent) spent surprisingly little time there. However, he took a keen interest in his project, and after each visit he left clear instructions as to the layout and development of the city. He stipulated that the streets be laid out in a grid pattern and that the houses conform to a specified style, with a veranda and covered passages to ameliorate the climate. In 1822, he implemented the Raffles Town Plan, designating areas to the four different ethnic groups: European, Chinese, Malay, and Indian. As in Java, Raffles was interested in the welfare of local people and set up wise and compassionate rule, promoting the education of the native Malay population.

His life, like that of many others who lived in the tropics, including his children, was cut short prematurely. He returned to England in 1824, and two years later died of a brain tumor. Before his death he was instrumental in founding the first zoological gardens in the world in London; he is also remembered as a great friend of William Wilberforce and the anti-slavery movement.

Although barely remembered in the land of his birth, Sir Stamford Raffles is widely commemorated in Singapore. There is a boulevard, a school, a college, a shopping mall, a golf club, and a lighthouse named after him. A bronze statue, saved during the Japanese occupation, is displayed in Empress Place, with a copy at Raffles Landing Site at Boat Quay in the Civic Center.

## Development

British political control went hand in hand with trade and Singapore continued to flourish in the nineteenth century. In 1826 the island was combined with Penang and Malacca to form the Straits Settlements, ruled by the Governor of Bengal, and

become their capital in 1832. From 1851 to 1858, they were the responsibility of the Governor General of India, after which they were run directly from London through the India Office. In 1867 they became a Crown Colony of the British Empire.

Economically Singapore grew from strength to strength, owing much to the rubber industry in Malaya and the opening of the Suez Canal in 1869. Western investments, banking, and business practices brought their advantages. The end of the century saw Singapore at the hub of international trade in the region. While the Malays resented and periodically rebelled against the British, Singapore remained politically calm and thrived as the area's primary port for the export of rubber and tin. The British authorities opened English-language primary schools, while the Chinese majority built Chinese-language schools.

Singapore was largely unaffected by the First World War, but after 1918 there was a dramatic rise in tin and rubber prices, creating great wealth for some. The strategic military importance of the island became more apparent as the British defended their colonial empire, and in 1922 it became the principal British military base in East Asia. Anti-Japanese sentiment among the Chinese population grew after Japan invaded Manchuria in 1931 and British officials outlawed anti-Japanese demonstrations and propaganda.

### Japanese Occupation

Japan invaded the Malay Peninsula in December 1941, and three months later the British surrendered Singapore, on February 14, 1942. The occupation of "Syonan," as the Japanese named Singapore, was brutal and savage. Thousands of expatriates, including women and children, were rounded up and put into camps for the duration of the war. Many never survived the starvation, disease, and

cruel punishments, and Allied prisoners of war were tortured and imprisoned in the notorious Changi jail. Near the causeway linking Singapore to Malaysia is the Kranji War Memorial to the Allied troops who died during the war. It is worth visiting this hillside cemetery with its 4,400 white gravestones not only for its peace and serenity but for the service held there every year on Remembrance Day to commemorate the dead. You can also visit the Changi chapel and museum (currently under restoration), the Battlebox at Fort Canning (where you can walk through the former British command center telling the story of the Singapore's fall), Bukit Chandu and the former Ford factory where the British surrendered unconditionally to the Japanese army.

Three years after the island's capitulation, the Japanese forces formerly surrendered on August 14, 1945. This momentous event ended one of the most painful periods in Singapore's history. What is often forgotten in the West is the suffering of the Singaporean Chinese. Some 50,000 men between the ages of eighteen and fifty, labeled "undesirables" by the Japanese, were arrested and summarily executed. Known as "*sook ching*" (the purge through cleansing), the most notable locations were Changi Beach, Punggol Point, and Sentosa. In Esplanade Park you can see the monument to Lim Bo Seng, a prominent Chinese businessman and resistance fighter. He was arrested by the Kempeitai, the Japanese Secret Police, and endured months of torture, never once betraying his comrades. His family paid with their lives.

Many older Singaporeans have long memories and find it difficult to forget and, especially, to forgive.

Like China and Korea, Singapore is still demanding that Japanese history textbooks state clearly what took place during the occupation of their countries. So far, their demands have not been heeded.

The younger generation take a more pragmatic view, realizing that the world has changed in the last sixty years. They welcome Japanese investment and technology, as well as the large number of Japanese expatriates who now live in the country. With a population of around 34,000, the Japanese have established their own primary and secondary schools, as well as the Japan–Singapore Association.

### Independence

After the war, Singapore's fortunes were inextricably bound up with those of Malaya. Despite calls for a unified Malay Peninsula, Britain resisted and dissolved the Straits Settlements, and made Singapore a Crown Colony in 1946. In the early 1950s the government of Singapore consisted of a British-appointed governor and a legislative council whose members were mostly wealthy Chinese businessmen. Primary education in Singapore's four main languages was introduced, but the British failure to defend Singapore during the war led to the rise of nationalist and anti-colonial feeling. Student and labor unrest grew as the pressure for self-rule increased. Reluctant to cede control, Britain finally granted Singapore full

self-government in 1959 with Lee Kuan Yew of the People's Action Party (PAP) elected as prime minister at the age of thirty-five. Lee introduced a new flag, a new national anthem, and made English, Chinese, Malay, and Tamil the official languages. In favor of a federation with Malaya, he signed the Malaysia Agreement, bringing Singapore into the newly created Federation of Malaysia four years later, when Malaya gained independence.

Over the decades the Chinese had worked hard, assumed managerial positions, and prospered, not only in Malaya but also in Singapore. This led to resentment by the Malays, and from the beginning there were political and racial tensions in the Federation. The Malay states were concerned that the power and influence of the largely Chinese population of Singapore would dominate the new Federation. After much agonizing and wrangling, Singapore was expelled, and on August 9, 1965, the Lion City became an independent republic. Facing a  future filled with uncertainties, it first joined the United Nations and then the Commonwealth and said "goodbye" to the British who withdraw their forces in 1971. Today, August 9 is celebrated with a National Day Parade, fireworks, and an address by the prime minister.

Lee Kuan Yew promised the people of Singapore a government free of corruption and a single multicultural national identity; he also worked to expand trade. He fostered good relations with his neighbors so that in 1967 Singapore joined Indonesia,

Malaysia, the Philippines, and Thailand in the
Association of Southeast Asian Nations (ASEAN).

## LEE KUAN YEW

Lee Kuan Yew was born in Singapore in 1923, a
third-generation descendant of immigrants from
Guangdong province. He studied law at Cambridge
University, England, and in 1954 he formed the
People's Action Party (PAP).

Most historians recognize that it was Lee's personal
vision, energy, and drive that turned Singapore

into the Asian
powerhouse that
it is today. Within
a few years of
independence, the
economy grew and
manufacturing
prospered. The
port facilities (its
deep-water harbor
being Singapore's
only natural asset and strategically placed to be the
distribution center for the rest of Asia) soon rivaled
those of London and New York.

Unlike many other countries in the region, the
wealth from the rapid economic growth filtered down
to the poorest in society. Lee was determined that
obedience to the rule of law would stifle corruption—
something that still bedevils the region. He also
believed passionately in equality of opportunity, no
matter one's ethnic origins.

Lee's vision of a prosperous, multiracial society has paid off handsomely: Singapore has a highly educated population, one of the highest literacy rates in the world, and excellent health care, social security, and transportation systems. Many citizens own their own homes in the brightly colored high-rise apartment blocks of the Housing Development Board (HDB).

Although Lee Kuan Yew officially retired in 1990 to assume the post of senior minister in the Singapore cabinet, he continued to influence the PAP until his death in 2015. His son, Lee Hsien Loong, followed as prime minister.

## SOCIAL CHANGE

At the time of independence the Chinese were the largest ethnic group, represented in all strata of society but dominating politics and government. The Malays worked in the civil service, as policemen, servants, or laborers, and Indians were predominantly shopkeepers or laborers.

The vision of a multiethnic society was not easy to achieve and in 1964–5, prior to the expulsion from the Federation of Malaysia, tension between the Chinese and the Malay underclass population boiled over. Fomented by extremist groups from Kuala Lumpur, race riots between Malay and Chinese youths led to many deaths.

Following independence, the government freed up the labor market by passing laws that gave employers more hiring and firing power; at the same time, workers received sick leave and unemployment benefits for the first time. Birth rates rose, and the

Family Planning and Population Board began to offer clinical services, education, and incentives such as priority housing and education in exchange for voluntary sterilization.

### The Housing Development Board

To raise living conditions and break down ethnic barriers, the new Housing Development Board (HDB) built high-rise apartment complexes and relocated lower-income citizens. The complexes

featured schools, shops, and recreation areas. Many families used their compulsory contributions to the Central Provident Fund to buy apartments. Legislative support came in the form of the Land Acquisition Act set up in 1967 to compulsorily acquire private land for public housing or other development programs. It enabled the HDB to clear squatters and slums and in their place build new and comfortable HDB apartments. The process was not without criticism, however. With the destruction of the *kampongs* (villages), some older Singaporeans struggled to live in the apartments and mourned the loss of their pigs and chickens and the close communities to which they had once belonged. Likewise, the enforced ethnic mix of the HDB complexes broke down traditional units that had been a feature of *kampong* life. To visit the last surviving *kampong*, you will have to take a "bumboat" (a small water taxi) from Changi Port Ferry Terminal to the island of Pulau Ubin (see page 121).

Yet, in the process housing went from Third World squalor to First World standards. Today, about 79 percent of Singaporeans live in HDB flats compared with only 9 percent in 1960 when the HDB was established. The government supports the public housing program by providing financial assistance for the funding of housing development and other activities. This is one of the few successful examples of the great modernist architect Le Corbusier's dream of the high-density city of the future.

**The Central Development Fund**
Singapore's compulsory social security savings scheme, the Central Provident Fund (CPF), was founded in 1955 and is an important engine of social change. Originally employees deposited a predetermined portion of their income into a tax-exempt account, which the employer matched. Today the rate of contribution is variable, and this adjustment is used by the government as an economic regulatory tool. The percentage average is 57 percent of someone's total wage with the employee paying a 20 percent contribution. The CPF is a comprehensive savings plan that has provided many working Singaporeans with security and confidence in their old age. Its overall scope and benefits encompass retirement, health care, home ownership, family protection, and asset enhancement.

CPF savings earn interest. Savings in the ordinary account earn a minimum interest rate of 2.5 percent per annum (in 2018 it averaged 3.5 percent), while savings in the special savings for old age contingencies and medisave accounts earn additional interest of 1.5 percentage points above the prevailing ordinary account interest rate. The most significant social outcome of the CPF is that most Singaporeans are able to buy their own homes.

In the 1970s emphasis on education raised living standards, reduced poverty, and blurred class lines. Most families occupied, and many owned, HDB apartments. The command of English and technical or professional skills marked the upwardly mobile.

The 1980s saw a growing need for manpower and the state responded by expanding vocational training and encouraging more women to work. An important element of this recruitment drive was the education of women. This transformed the workplace, and today Singapore is unique in Asia in terms of women's presence and position in the workforce, having, according to the World Economic Forum, a Gender Parity score in 2017 of 0.70 (the highest being 1). This compares favorably with the UK, which has 0.77 and the USA which has 0.701. While this policy has boosted household incomes, it has had the unwelcome consequence of lowering the birth-rate, and the government has launched a pro-birth campaign, offering tax rebates and day care subsidies for the third child as well as extended mandatory paid paternity leave and cash for babies (the amount increases exponentially from 14,000 Singapore dollars, or S$, for the first child to S$ 28,000 for the fifth).

To ensure a balanced racial mix within HDB estates and to foster greater racial harmony, the ethnic integration policy was introduced. This sets limits on the total percentage an ethnic group can occupy a block or neighborhhood. As a consequence, even though people are free to buy and sell flats, they can only do so if the ethnic percentage allowance is not exceeded. The HDB continues to work with other government ministries to provide social facilities such as community centers and neighborhood parks. Towns are planned with precinct spaces such as amphitheaters and pavilions to give residents more opportunities to interact with one another for a more cohesive community.

## LAW AND ORDER

The country's stability has come at a price. Many critics would argue that Singapore is over governed. Once known affectionately by tourists as "fine city," most visitors are surprised that heavy fines are levied on those who chew gum without a doctor's prescription. You cannot spit in public places, jaywalk within fifty meters of a crossing zone, or drop litter; nor can you feed pigeons or walk about nude in your home without drawing the curtains. Smoking is banned in most restaurants and there is a fine for not flushing a public lavatory after use. As for vandalism, the penalty can sometimes involve caning—anything from three to eight strokes. In fact, caning is widely used as a punishment and a deterrent, although neither women nor men over fifty are struck. Recently, there has been a movement against physical punishment in school and at home; however in both cases it remains legal. Trial by jury was initially retained after independence for murder, but with too few convictions, in the view of the government, it was abolished in 1969. In the 1980s, community policing was introduced and small neighborhood posts were opened. By the end of the decade 15 percent of police officers were women.

The 1990s saw the judiciary demonstrate its constitutional independence by ruling against

the government in many political and civil rights cases. Although government officials intimidate political opponents and censor the press, they make no attempt to reverse rulings, or to remove or intimidate judges. Today Singapore remains a tightly ruled society but maintains what it sees as a fair balance between openness and control. It is said to have the best judicial system in Southeast Asia.

## POLITICAL LIFE

The People's Action Party (PAP) remains overwhelmingly dominant, thanks both to its popularity and harsh measures to limit opposition campaigning. Voting is compulsory, and the PAP won 83 of the 89 seats in the 2015 general election. In contrast, the main opposition party, the Workers' Party, took only six.

The authoritarian style of Lee Kuan Yew and his successors has all but suppressed political opposition. Life is made difficult for those who oppose the PAP; there is little political debate in the media and many parliamentary candidates are returned to power without opposition. The Workers' Party accused the PAP of using defamation laws to stop candidates running in 2015 and putting neighborhoods that voted for them at the bottom of the list for public housing. In 2017, Reporters Without Borders put Singapore 151st for press freedom.

While this may seem oppressive to the Western visitor, it is worth remembering that for more than fifty years PAP rule has meant wise, efficient government. The people's standard of living has steadily improved, with Singapore having the highest rate of home ownership and national savings in the world, coupled with respect for law and order. This is a multiracial society that is understandably risk-averse when it comes to untested government.

Discussing these matters with Singaporeans is not recommended, as the government is sensitive to criticism by foreigners. Furthermore, Lee Kuan Yew felt, and his successors feel, that the West has given up on its own values—pointing to drug abuse, crime, and violence in Western society and the associated breakdown of family life and homelessness. If a Singaporean does venture any views on politics, the comment will probably be that politics is best left to the politicians, while ordinary people get on with the important business of making money.

## URBAN DEVELOPMENT

The first generation of political leaders was determined to change Singapore into a modern and dynamic metropolis. Far-sighted and with long-term urban plans, they invested money in urbanization projects, predominantly in the HDB public housing project whose key aims were to avoid ghettos, resettle the people, and clear the land. All of this came under the Urban Redevelopment Authority (URA), which, in the twenty-first century, has given Singaporeans clean air, flowing traffic, a good infrastructure, and a comfortable life.

The government owns 90 percent of the land and believes that it has consistently improved the people's quality of life, working toward an ecologically sustainable urban system. This does not mean, however, that all development has been welcomed. The "Save Bukit Brown" campaign lobbied to halt the development of the heritage site to make way for housing and to build an eight-lane highway to alleviate peak hour traffic congestion. The largest Chinese cemetery outside China, Bukit Brown is a 230-hectare site with more than 100,000 graves, the oldest dating back to 1822. It is a much-loved area for hikers, bird watchers, and those in search of some peace and serenity.

Land reclamation has been key to Singapore's industrialization and the island has expanded by

about 25 percent over the last two centuries. Most of the southern coast has been altered as well as stretches of the northeastern coast, with waters between small offshore islands filled in to create larger areas. Marina Bay is the best place to visit to appreciate the scale of this project. Begun in 1969 and finished in 2008 with the building of the Marina Barrage, the waterfront site has been extended by 360 hectares and transformed into a new freshwater Marina Reservoir. Now it hosts—to name a few—the ArtScience Museum, the F1 Pit Building, the Gardens by the Bay, the Theatres on the Bay, and the iconic Marina Bay Sands Hotel.

Such systematic and sustained development has resulted, over the years, in the loss of 95 percent of Singapore's mangroves and most of its coral reefs. Aware of the cost to the environment, the government introduced the Sustainable Singapore Blueprint in 2015.

# VALUES & ATTITUDES

## COMMON ASIAN VALUES

Singapore is home to three of Asia's great cultures—Chinese, Malay, and Indian—and, although they each have their own distinct norms, values, and religions, many of these are held in common. As a consequence, a Singaporean Chinese, Malay, and Indian may well understand each other better than a Westerner, and this could explain in part why it is such a successful multicultural society.

For instance, a group's or an individual's dignity is to be respected at all times, and anything that undermines it is taboo. The "loss of face," in other words anything that severely embarrasses the group or individual, must be avoided at all costs. Furthermore, all three ethnic groups, while strongly advocating equal opportunities, also firmly believe in a hierarchical society, one that gives deference to age and learning, where status is earned and not simply inherited, and where position in turn brings responsibility.

Relationships are important and have to be cultivated over a long period of time. For this reason, Singaporeans prefer doing business with people they know, such as family and friends, or school and university contacts. Thus, when there are problems, businesses first look to their suppliers and customers for help rather than to the contract and their lawyers, as is often the case in the West.

Outside a business context, Singaporeans can be synchronic in their approach to time, and they consider social time commitments to be desirable rather than important. One thing at a time is not the custom; instead many things are done at once and time is elastic. With this comes the frequent changing of details and plans. Westerners who focus on the arrangement rather than the relationship will find this frustrating.

The Singaporeans tend not to speak their minds and as a result can appear indirect and ambiguous in their approach. Not wishing to upset or embarrass anyone by disagreeing, an affirmative answer or reply might not mean anything more than "I hear you." Similarly, Singaporeans are seldom direct when giving bad news; they do not seek to deceive but wish to avoid damaging the relationship or causing the hearer distress.

## RELIGION

Singapore is a secular state that rightly prides itself on its religious tolerance; its citizens are free to worship as they see fit. In fact, religion plays an important role in society and everyday life. There are no bank holidays; rather public holidays celebrate state occasions (such as National Day) and religious festivals (such as Deepavali, or Divali). To a great extent the different ethnic communities are defined by their religion, and many of their characteristic values, attitudes, and customs are rooted in traditional belief.

## The Chinese

To the Chinese, religion is first and foremost about easing one's passage through life. Their belief system is a pragmatic combination of three distinct religious philosophies—Taoism, Buddhism, and Confucianism. Taken together, these address a range of spiritual, intellectual, and social needs and have sustained the Chinese people for thousands of years.

The Singapore Chinese have tended not to convert to Islam as frequently as they have to Christianity, especially the Protestant evangelical sects that are prevalent and popular on the island. This is in contrast to their adaptation of Malay cuisine, and may have something to do with Islamic strictures against drinking alcohol and eating certain foods beloved by the Chinese, such as pork. Conversion to another religion can cause Chinese parents and grandparents great alarm for fear their children and descendants will no longer carry out the correct funeral rites or continue the worship and veneration of the ancestors.

### Taoism

Taoism is essentially about living in harmony with the natural world. The *Tao Te Ching* and *Zhuangzi* are the two principal texts, the first supposedly written by the sage Laozi, or Lao Tsu. The Chinese word *tao* means "way." It sees the universe as being divided into two opposing yet complementary aspects, the primal forces of Yin and Yang. These polarities are illustrated by the Yin–Yang symbol. The two swirling shapes inside the circle teach about change—the only constant factor in the universe.

Each state contains within it the seed of its opposite, toward which it is moving; hence there is a small black spot in the white swirl, and a corresponding white spot in the black swirl. One tradition states that Yin (or Ying, the dark side) represents the breath that formed the earth. Yang (the light side) symbolizes the breath that formed the heavens. The most common view is that Yin represents aspects of the feminine, being soft, cool, calm, introspective, and healing, and Yang the masculine, being hard, hot, energetic, moving, and sometimes aggressive. Another view has Yin representing the night and Yang the day.

This principle of balancing forces is embedded in Chinese thought. Everything must be in equilibrium—in the world, the nation, and the human body—for it to prosper. According to this belief, a root cause of illness in the body is the imbalance between Yin (cool) and Yang (hot) foods. Similarly, traditional relationships must be kept harmonious, for example, between father and son, husband and wife, a ruler and his subjects, and between nation-state and nation-state. In this way Taoism, although itself an irreverent and quietist philosophy, can complement the conservative rigidity of Confucian teaching.

Chinese belief embraces a panoply of deities, ghosts, and devils, and temples are sited and built strictly according to the rules of Feng Shui, so that they will be free from evil. Feng Shui, the ancient art of geomancy, holds that the proper alignment of walls, furniture, and objects will greatly enhance the flow of *chi*—energy, or the life force—and bring prosperity to the prudent occupants of the building or the worshipers at the temple. The visitor to a Chinese temple will be aware of this as he steps over a curb designed to trip up evil spirits and passes through doors painted with images of terrifying gods and guarded by two lions, female and male, representing Yin and Yang. When entering the inner courtyard, the visitor is obliged to remove his shoes. Although the Chinese are reverential when visiting their temples, they also see them as communal spaces where people come together to meet, to exchange ideas, and maybe to gossip amid the chants, gongs, bells, and the perfumed aroma of incense.

The oldest Chinese temple in Singapore is Thian Hock Keng in Telok Ayer Street. It was built around 1821 to worship and thank Mazu, the goddess of the sea. It is richly decorated with colored tiles and lacquer work and is in the standard form of three

halls. If you are interested in Chinese religion and folklore, a visit to the Tiger Balm Gardens or Haw Par Villa, built in 1935, is also recommended. The Ten Courts of Hell and the Twenty-four Filial Exemplars are just some of the attractions in this unique and rather alarming theme park.

### Buddhism

Buddhism addresses the problem of human suffering and offers a way to resolve it. Its founder, Siddhartha Gautama, the Buddha (or "Enlightened One"), was born a Hindu prince in about 563 BCE in what today is Nepal. His teachings spread far beyond India to flourish and grow in China, Korea, Japan, and Southeast Asia. Born into great wealth, Siddhartha Gautama knew nothing of suffering or poverty during his childhood. At the age of twenty-nine, he renounced the luxury and wealth of the palace and embarked on a quest for true knowledge. After first embracing extreme ascetic practices, he reverted to "the middle way" of meditation until, at the age of thirty-four, seated beneath a banyan, or bo, tree he experienced enlightenment.

Initially, the Buddha confronted the excesses of the Brahmin priests whom he had seen lusting after wealth and power, neither of which led to happiness in this life or the next. He taught that in order to attain *nirvana*, or true enlightenment, one had first to recognize the Four Noble Truths. They are that life is suffering; there is a cause of suffering—our attachment to notions and things; there is an end to suffering—our attachment is, in essence, empty; and that the way to achieve the end of suffering is by following the Eightfold Path. This depends on right thought or view, right intention, right speech, right action, right livelihood, right effort, right mindfulness, and right *samadhi* or concentration, and are represented in the eight spokes of the *dharmachakra* (dharma wheel).

Buddhism later split into two major schools: Theravada ("teaching of the elders")—also known, pejoratively, as Hinayana (or "lesser vehicle")— which teaches individuals how to attain personal enlightenment; and Mahayana (the "greater vehicle"), which teaches the Great Compassion—the practitioner delays his own *nirvana* until all beings have been liberated. Both strands of Buddhism are present in Singapore, although the latter is more popular.

## Confucian Philosophy

Not so much a religion as an ethical system, the philosophy of Confucianism has shaped Chinese civilization for over two thousand years. The scholar-sage Confucius was born in around 551 BCE. He devoted his life to the study and teaching of the Chinese classics, and his writings are mainly comments on these. The origin of things lies in the union of Yin and Yang. Human relationships are hierarchical. Confucius emphasized personal virtue, promotion on merit by scholarship, devotion to the family, and justice. His precepts dealt with morality in human affairs and continue to form a practical guide for daily life. They include obedience to authority, adherence to one's social position, respect for the elderly, and the veneration of ancestors. They also stress the virtues of education, hard work, thrift, loyalty, and harmony. Unlike contemporary Western value systems, Confucianism does not give overriding importance to the rights of the individual; it stresses the needs of the group, and the duties and obligations of the individual.

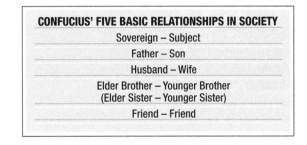

| CONFUCIUS' FIVE BASIC RELATIONSHIPS IN SOCIETY |
| :---: |
| Sovereign – Subject |
| Father – Son |
| Husband – Wife |
| Elder Brother – Younger Brother (Elder Sister – Younger Sister) |
| Friend – Friend |

*Confucianism in Practice*
From infancy onward, Chinese children know
that they belong to a tightly knit group and they
are taught never to dishonor the group or bring
shame upon it. If a member of the family needs
help, whether it is financial or moral, the rest of the
family will come to their aid. Taking in orphaned
nieces or nephews, rescuing a brother or sister
from bankruptcy, and supporting a family member
who is sick and unemployed are all part of family
obligation. The child who places his or her needs
before others is considered amoral, untrustworthy,
and something of a social misfit.

These Confucian values, first taught in the
home, are later reinforced at school, often in a
practical manner—such as designating a group to be
responsible for books for the whole class, or serving
the rest of the children at lunch, or clearing up after
lunch or at the end of the school day.

Obligation comes in many forms, but none more
so than in the care of elderly parents who have given
life and nurture to their children. The responsibility
to ensure they have a contented old age, free from
want and safe in the knowledge that the veneration

due to them
will be carried
out after their
deaths, falls to
the adult child,
especially the
eldest son. It used
to be the norm
in Singapore that
three generations
would live under
one roof, but this
less the case now.

Education is
highly valued, not only because it ensures a good
career and, hopefully, a prosperous one, but because
it is essential for the development of individual
potential, which enhances the whole group.

Unlike Western cultures where rugged
individualism and self-assertiveness are encouraged
from an early age, Singapore is most definitely
not an "I" society. Moreover, it suffers none of
the Western unease with status and hierarchy.
It positively encourages the paying of respect to
people of higher status, whether it means venerating
age, because of the wisdom it has brought, or
learning, because of the long years of study needed
to achieve a particular professional position.
Similarly, the boss is revered in a Singaporean
company and is given the loyalty that is his due. In
return his staff expect him to take a paternalistic
interest in their family as well as work-related
problems.

The government has adopted this paternalistic role and has harnessed Confucianism to create a more cohesive society, encouraging the three-tier family, filial piety, and education.

*Young People*
It is not difficult to see how Confucian values can create a dedicated, highly motivated, and responsible workforce with an enhanced sense of commitment and loyalty. It is also true to say, however, that some young Singaporeans consider these values irrelevant in the modern world. In fact, the government became so concerned by this trend that it carried out a survey to discover the values held by young Singaporeans. Reassuringly, the overwhelming majority stated that filial piety, honesty, responsibility, and self-control were as important to them as they had been to their ancestors.

**The Malays**
About 99 percent of the Malay population in Singapore is Muslim. This was not always the case, as Buddhism and Hinduism were the earliest religious influences in the region. However, by the time Marco Polo visited Southeast Asia in 1292, Islam was well established, with mosques being built on the sites of former Buddhist and Hindu temples.

*Islam*
Islam is the monotheistic cousin to Judaism and Christianity. The word *Islam* means the active and voluntary submission to the will of God as revealed to the prophet Muhammad. Born in idol-worshiping

Mecca in the Arabian Peninsula c. 570 CE, Muhammad received the call in midlife to proclaim the worship of one God (Allah) in about 616. He established the first Islamic community in Medina after fleeing persecution in Mecca. Today both cities are holy to Muslims.

The holy book of Islam, recording the pure and uncorrupted word of God, was revealed to Muhammad by the angel Gabriel and is called the *Quran* (meaning "recitation"). It records, in non-chronological order, many of the stories found in the Bible, including Jesus, and contains a clear code of conduct governing aspects of daily life, such as dressing modestly, and the prohibition of gambling, drinking alcohol, eating of pork and other *haram* foods. The second-most important source of Islamic teaching is the *Hadith* ("tradition"), which forms the traditions and sayings of the Prophet. The fundamental duties that shape Muslim life are called the Five Pillars of the Faith.

---

### THE FIVE PILLARS OF ISLAM

**Affirmation:** the duty to recite the creed "There is no God but Allah, and Muhammad is the Messenger of God."

**Prayer:** the duty to worship God in prayer five times each day.

**Almsgiving:** the duty to distribute alms and to help the needy.

**Fasting:** self-purification and the duty to keep the fast of Ramadan.

**Pilgrimage:** the duty to make the pilgrimage, or *Hajj*, to the shrine of the Ka'aba at Mecca at least once in a lifetime.

If you are visiting Singapore during the month of Ramadan, do remember that all good Muslims, apart from the elderly, the very young, pregnant women, and nursing mothers, will be fasting. No food or drink may be taken between sunrise and sunset. Although the fast is seen as beneficial to health, it is regarded principally as a method of spiritual discipline and self-purification. By cutting oneself off from worldly comforts, even for a short time, a fasting person pleases Allah by gaining true sympathy with those who go hungry. Therefore, it would be the height of insensitivity to eat in the presence of someone you knew to be a Muslim, whether Indian or Malay, at this time.

It is forbidden for Muslim men and women to touch members of the opposite sex outside the immediate family, so do not automatically go to shake the hand of a colleague. Certain animals, such as pigs, dogs, and amphibians are considered unclean, so if you invite Malay friends to your house and you have dogs, it is a good idea to put them in another room for the duration of the visit. Remember a Muslim is strictly forbidden to come into contact with the nose, saliva, or hair of a dog, hence a Muslim taxi driver may refuse to take you if you are traveling with a dog.

Friday is the Muslim day of prayer, and you will see people making their way to the mosques dressed in their best clothes for the occasion, such as the male *songkok*, or black velvet hat. Commerce and industry usually allow Muslims to take an extended lunch on Friday so they can attend prayers; they will also provide a private space in the office for short daily prayers during the week.

Non-Muslims may visit mosques providing they are quiet and respectful and remember to take their shoes off before entering. Visitors should be modestly dressed, and women should have their arms, legs, and head covered. Of course, you should always ask permission before

taking any photographs. A good time to visit is between 9:00 a.m. and 12 noon, when the mosque is relatively quiet.

*Budi*

Malays have their own philosophical code of behavior, which is similar in some respects to Confucianism. This is known as Budi. According to its laws, the individual should have a pleasant disposition, show respect for other people, especially the elderly, and always be courteous toward them. To show love and affection to one's parents is also important, as is the maintenance of harmony in the family and society as a whole.

**The Indians**

The Indian community is not defined by one religion. Over half its members are Hindu, while others may be Muslim or Sikh, or—especially those from Southern India—Christian.

## Hinduism

Hinduism originated in North India about four thousand years ago. Superficially it embraces many apparent contradictions, differing forms of worship, and a profusion of divinities. Underlying this wide variety, however, is the belief in one supreme and ultimate reality, Brahman, which is unknowable in itself but whose attributes are revealed through a plethora of gods and goddesses. The Hindu trinity symbolizes its three key aspects: creation (Brahma), preservation (Vishnu), and destruction (Shiva). One of the most popular gods is Ganesh, the elephant god. He is the god of good luck and the remover of obstacles, and no undertaking, apart from funerals, is contemplated without involving and making an offering to him. As long as a Hindu identifies himself with the Hindu faith, accepts as sacred the ancient Vedic literature, and recognizes the caste system, he is assured a place in Hindu society.

Hinduism has several sacred works, the oldest of which are the Vedic scriptures, the tales, songs, and ceremonial instructions of the Indo-European Aryan settlers in the Indian subcontinent. There are four *Vedas* (Sanskrit for "knowledge"): the *Rig Veda*, probably the oldest religious book in the world, compiled between 1500 BCE and 900 BCE; the *Sama Veda*, a collection of sacred songs; the *Yajur Veda*, used by priests in the performance of their religious duties; and the *Atharva Veda*, a book of incantations. These, together with the Hindu Epics, the *Ramayana* and the *Mahabharata*—the tales of early Aryan heroes, the most famous of which is the *Bhagavad Gita*—contain the basic beliefs of modern Hinduism.

Hindus believe that all living beings have a soul, or *atman*. Life is a series of rebirths and reincarnations until the soul, by its virtuous behavior, is released from the cycle of birth and death. An individual's spiritual progress is determined by *karma* (the law of consequence, or fate), and by *dharma* (the obligation to accept one's condition and perform the duties appropriate to it). As no one can escape the duties of *dharma*, this naturally reinforces the Indian caste system. Hindus therefore believe that in this life they get what they deserve; whatever happens, it is the consequence of behavior in their previous lives. Personal duty is all-important in the Hindu faith.

### Christianity

Although Christianity is not a religion traditionally associated with Southeast Asia, 19 percent of the country consider themselves members of the faith, making it the second-largest religion in the country in 2015 (compared to 33 percent Buddhist, 14 percent Muslim, 11 percent Taoist, and 5 percent

Hindu). The majority are Protestant, but the array of denominations is great, from Eastern Orthodox to Roman Catholic, Lutheran to Presbyterian. The Anglican diocese of Singapore has twenty-six parishes and the Cathedral of St. Andrews is the largest in the country, having been built in 1856.

The rise of Christianity is probably best explained by Lee Kuan Yew, not himself a Christian. In an interview in 2009 he said, "You see most Chinese here are Buddhists or Taoist ancestor worshippers . . . and these youngsters, the educated ones, Western-educated especially, read Western books and Western culture and they begin to question . . . what is this mumbo-jumbo, the ancestors and so on? . . . and they have got groups, Christian groups who go out and evangelize. They catch them in their teens when they're malleable and open to suggestions . . . . My granddaughter is one of them. She's now twenty-eight."

## EDUCATION

Education is highly regarded in Singapore and the introduction of free compulsory education transformed the social scene. Government reforms raised the educational standards in state schools and narrowed the gap in attainment between social groups. Now their education results are the envy of the world, and competition is great. Parents will move home and spend large sums of money on private tuition to ensure their children gain top marks. There are more than 300 privately owned educational institutions and 28 International schools that are only accessible to Singapore nationals under special permission of the Ministry of Education. The six universities are heavily subsidized, with the National University of Singapore and the Nanyan Technological University ranking 12th and 13th in the 2016 QS World University Rankings.

## A GOAL-DRIVEN SOCIETY

Younger Singaporeans of all backgrounds prize success, and a goal-oriented approach is replacing the traditional relationship-based dealings of their parents in the workplace. It is often considered a "masculine" society, driven by competition, achievement, and success. Socially, this can be seen in a form of status anxiety known as *kiasu*—a Hokkien world meaning the "fear of losing," or, in other words, missing out. If your neighbor is hurrying to buy the latest electronic wizardry, you had better rush to do so too, in case it sells out. You don't want to be left behind. This is possibly why most young Singaporeans pursue without shame the Five Cs: cash, condo, car, credit card, and country club!

# chapter three

# CUSTOMS & TRADITIONS

## FESTIVALS AND HOLIDAYS

If you enjoy festivals and celebrations, you will love Singapore. Owing to its rich multicultural heritage different festivals are celebrated throughout the calendar year, the main events being Chinese New Year and the Hungry Ghosts festival, Deepavali, the Festival of Lights, Hari Raya Puasa, and Christmas. Some festivals are also public holidays.

| PUBLIC HOLIDAYS | |
|---|---|
| **New Year's Day** | 1 January |
| **Chinese New Year** | January or February* |
| **Hari Raya Haji** | January* |
| **Good Friday** | Around April* |
| **Labor Day** | 1 May |
| **Vesak Day** | April, May, or June* |
| **Singapore National Day** | 9 August |
| **Deepavali** | October or November* |
| **Hari Raya Puasa** | End of Ramadan* |
| **Christmas Day** | 25 December |
| * Dates vary according to the different lunar calendars. | |

## Chinese New Year

Chinese New Year, also known as the Lunar New Year, is the longest and most important festive period for the Chinese community. It begins on the second new moon after the winter solstice, usually between mid-January and mid-February, and lasts fifteen days. Everyday life seems to come to a halt and it is common for non-Chinese Singaporeans to go away on holiday at this time. Everywhere you go you hear the beating of drums and clanging of cymbals. Most shopping malls offer discounts and are decorated in the auspicious colors of red and gold with tiny mandarin trees (that symbolize prosperity) flanking the entrances. The main hub of activity is Chinatown, with its great lanterns festooning the streets and famous lion and dragon

dances, but you can also go to the Marina Bay floating platform to enjoy the River Hongbao. This is a colorful extravaganza of fireworks and giant lanterns and other activities, from amusement rides to street performances. The most famous celebration, however, is the Chingay parade, Asia's largest street event, which features floats, lion

dances, acrobats, children, beauty queens, and cultural shows from different lands.

The festival itself, is preceded by a flurry of household activity: cleaning, to sweep out bad luck, cooking special regional foods of mainland China, plus shopping trips for new clothes. The celebration proper starts on New Year's Eve, when families are invited to a grand reunion dinner at the paternal home, and children pay respects to their parents. Candles burn all night and homage is paid to the ancestors. The evening's activities reaffirm the family's identity and closeness. The noisy part begins at midnight, when drums and kettles are banged and windows are thrown open to usher out the old year and usher in the new.

Next morning it is the custom for children to serve their parents tea, and they in turn give them *hongbao*, red envelopes containing money. Family and friends visit each other over the next few days, except for the third day, which is dedicated to remembering and venerating the ancestors. On the fourth day businessmen usually hold a grand banquet for their employees.

### Giving Hongbao

The Mandarin word *hongbao* (in Hokkein, *angbao*) means "red packet," and is said to bring good luck to children and unmarried adults. Visiting foreigners who are married should give *hongbao* to their hosts' children. Also, on the Chinese New Year a foreign manager should give *hongbao* to his staff. Check with your colleagues on the appropriate amount.

## Vesak Day

The most important event for the Buddhist community in Singapore takes place on the full moon of the fourth lunar month, usually in April, May, or June. It commemorates the birth and enlightenment of the Buddha and his entry into *nirvana*. The various Buddhist sects celebrate Vesak Day in different ways. In the temples, saffron-robed priests chant *sutras* while devotees pray, meditate, and make offerings. As an act of compassion, in accordance with the Buddha's teaching, captured birds and animals are set free, and alms are given to the poor. The celebration concludes with a candlelit procession through the streets.

## Dragon Boat Festival

The Dragon Boat Festival falls on the fifth day of the fifth lunar month, usually in May or June. It commemorates the suicide in the third century BC of Qu Yuan, a respected poet and incorruptible minister of the King of Chu, who threw himself into the Mei Lo River after being banished by the King. Today, lively competitions between long, thin "dragon boats" are held at Bedock Reservoir, the Kallang River, and the Garden by the Bay Marina Channel. These races are said to represent the local fishermen who rowed out to try to rescue Qu Yuan from the man-eating fish. In the same way, Singaporeans eat rice dumplings wrapped in bamboo leaves called Ma Chang that represent the rice thrown to the fish in the hope they might leave the poet alone. Taoist ceremonies are performed on the boats to bless and "awaken" them before the race, and to induce them to "repose" afterward.

**Hungry Ghosts Festival**

The Hungry Ghosts festival takes place in the seventh Chinese lunar month, between July and August. It is thought that the restless spirits of the dead roam the earth at this time and need to be appeased with gifts of food and money. This is the most inauspicious time of the year. No marriages take place, children are discouraged from staying out late at night, and it is considered unlucky to buy property or close a deal during the festival. The month is punctuated by dinners of many courses, Chinese street operas, auctions, and noisy celebrations to pacify the ghosts. These take place in large marquees set up in housing estates or open fields, and the ghosts are said to sit in the front rows! Bonfires can be seen all over Singapore, burning offerings of "hell" money and luxury paper goods such as cars, houses, and cell phones to the spirits. Most food is laid out on altars, but offerings are often found along footpaths and beside trees.

**National Day**
Singapore's independence is celebrated on August 9 and culminates in the National Day Parade, which is held at Marina Bay with crowds of more than 25,000 spectators. Celebrations include the Presidential Gun Salute, the parade itself, and the evening fireworks. All groups are represented—the ethnic communities, schoolchildren, civil organizations, and the armed forces—and outside the windows of most housing estates the Singaporean flag is displayed. Each year there is a different theme, and there are weeks of practice beforehand. Tickets are available for the dress rehearsal.

**Lantern Festival**
Usually falling in September, on the fifteenth day of the eighth Chinese lunar month, when the moon is supposed to be brighter and fuller than at any other time of the year, this is the harvest festival of ancient China, celebrating the legend of the moon goddess, Chang-O. Also known as the Mooncake Festival, it is celebrated by the eating of mooncakes, which today come in a variety of flavors, from the traditional

sweet pastries made with flour, oil, and lotus seed to snowskin versions filled with chocolate, green tea, rose, and the like. At night, children carry brightly colored lanterns in the shape of birds and animals in a parade. A special feature of the festival is the dragon dance, where an enormous dragon head and body, supported by a team of dancers, weaves its way around the streets collecting money on its route.

Among the legends associated with mooncakes is the overthrowing of the Mongol Yuan dynasty by Chinese rebels, who sent secret messages to each other hidden in the mooncakes.

### Deepavali

The Festival of Lights, Deepavali, or Diwali, is celebrated at the darkest time of the year, usually in October or November, and marks the start of the

Hindu New Year. The festival celebrates the defeat of the demon Narakasura by Lord Krishna, or the triumph of light over darkness and good over evil. It is a time of rejoicing and renewal in Hindu homes. Oil lamps are lit, garlands of jasmine placed at the family altar, and family and friends visit each other. Before the festival itself, houses are cleaned and new clothes bought. This is the time for the closing of accounts, for giving gifts, and offering worship to Lakshmi, the goddess of prosperity. Throughout Little India there is a blaze of light and sound from temples, night bazaars, and performances of traditional Indian songs and dances.

**Hari Raya Puasa (Eid al-Fitr)**
The date of this Muslim festival varies according to the lunar calendar and marks the end of the month-long fast of Ramadan when devout Muslims have neither drunk nor eaten during the hours of daylight. The celebration of the breaking of the fast begins with housecleaning, the purchase of new clothes and, of course, the preparation of a splendid meal. Dishes include the seasonal *Ketupat*, savory rice in woven palm leaves, plus *Lontong* rice rolls in banana leaves, and the ever popular *Nasi Padang*, which means "rice field" and is in fact plain boiled rice served with a selection of dishes, including curry and the famous Malay *Rendang*, a dry beef or chicken curry.

The celebrations last three days and in Gelyland Serai, the cultural heart of the Malay community, you can enjoy traditional Malay song and dance, food stalls, and festive bazaars. Families wear their best clothes, give green packets of money to children, and visit families, friends, and the local mosque.

### Christmas

Every year from the end of November to January 1, Singapore celebrates "Christmas in the Tropics." Orchard Road and Marina Bay are ablaze with great arches of street lighting, Christmas trees festoon the shopping malls, and festive-themed sets twinkle with fake snow. Shop windows are decorated, and many retailers offer promotions and discounts. At night there is entertainment along Orchard Road with choral groups and parade floats; the popular Zoukout dance festival takes place on Sentosa and the Christmas Wonderland fairground can be found at the Gardens by the Bay.

Christian families attend midnight mass and share a traditional Christmas dinner, but the nature of celebrations depends on regional and cultural variations.

### New Year's Eve

Singapore's largest countdown party takes place at Marina Bay on December 31. Here, the atmosphere is carnival-like and people gather to watch the firework display that begins at the stroke of midnight. If people are not hosting private parties or picnicking at Fort Canning and Mount Faber, they gather at places such as 1-Altitude or the Fullerton to gaze at the city in its blazing array of colors

### THE CHINESE LUNAR CALENDAR

Despite being highly Westernized, the lives of Chinese Singaporeans are still governed by many traditional beliefs, including Chinese astrology. These influence important life decisions such as births and marriages.

The Chinese lunar calendar is said to have been adopted in 2,698 BCE, and years are counted from that date onward, with some adjustments. It works a sixty-year-cycle divided into twelve sets of five years, each year being named after one of the animals of the Chinese Zodiac, for example, the Year of the Dog or the Year of the Monkey. Half the animals are domestic, and half are wild, reflecting the Yin–Yang balance. Within the sixty-year cycle, the most important birthday celebrations are the first and the sixtieth, when the individual is said to start a new life. After the sixtieth, birthdays are celebrated every ten years. Apart from these two key birthdays, the ages of 25, 29, 33, 36, and 66 are considered critical, and these, too, are occasions for celebration.

## BIRTHS
### Chinese

It is said that for the first thirty days after birth the mother's pores are open and cold air can enter the body. Consequently, new Chinese mothers may be forbidden to go outdoors or take a shower or bath. Diet will be high in Yang foods, including meat, eggs, and liver, and Yin foods may be avoided. Traditionally many mothers will eat specially prepared soups and broths containing pigs' feet and chicken. The great celebration of the baby's birth takes place after this month and, as with all Chinese festivities, it centers upon food. A large number of family and friends are invited to a party, especially for a first-born child, and hard-boiled eggs with red painted shells, a universal symbol of life, are given to the guests. In turn, the guests bring gifts such as baby clothes, usually in the propitious colors of red, pink, gold, or orange, and always in matching pairs. The colors in the West that are often associated with babies, such as white or blue, are symbols of death and are therefore taboo. Interestingly, the Chinese consider a baby to be one year old at birth.

### Malay

As with the Indian and Chinese communities, most Malay babies are now born in hospital and many traditional Malay practices associated with the birth of a child have had to be abandoned. The child's name is formally bestowed forty-four days after birth, although the name will already have been registered with the civil authorities. This religious ceremony takes place at home and is often followed by a party. There is no problem about the colors of gifts for the baby, and some people will give money, discreetly enclosed in an envelope.

### Indian
Every Hindu baby will have a horoscope drawn up at birth by the Brahmin priest; this will be consulted at major events in the child's life and is known as the *kundli*. The great celebration of the birth itself takes place twenty-eight days after the child has come into the world, when its name is whispered into the baby's ear by the father. This is followed by a visit to the temple by mother and child to give thanks for a safe delivery and for the baby's birth hair to be shaved off. Acceptable gifts are cuddly toys and baby outfits in cheerful colors, but again, avoid white.

## WEDDINGS
### Chinese
Weddings are celebrated in style in Singapore but the traditions will differ depending on the families' ancestral regions. Often now, the Chinese bride dresses in the traditional white wedding dress of the West during the day, and then changes into the lucky red or pink gown for the wedding banquet in the evening. The ceremony starts with the smartly dressed groom arriving in an elaborately pink and red decorated car to collect his bride. They then proceed to the groom's house where the bride is welcomed into her new family. First, the couple honor the household gods and pay their respects to the ancestors. Next, the all-important tea

ceremony, or *jin cha*, takes place with the bride and
groom offering the groom's seated parents a cup of
ceremonial tea. The father, as head of the family,
sips first and then his wife. In this way the bride
is accepted into her new family. The family then
give the bride *hongbao*, which may contain either
money or jewelry. At this point, all the relatives are
offered tea in turn according to their position in the
family, and the younger generation serve the bride
tea to welcome her. The couple then move on to
the bride's house where a similar tea ceremony is
performed.

The wedding banquet is usually vast, both in
terms of the number of guests invited and the
number of courses served. The bride and groom
visit each table where they are toasted. However,
some couples prefer to have a wedding buffet
during the day as it is less formal, usually less
expensive, and guests can dance or be entertained
after the meal.

Near the end of the celebrations, the couple—along with their families and friends—gather around their tables or on stage and drink a toast, raising their glasses and shouting as loud as they can "*yam seng!*" three times: first for a blissful marriage, the second for eternal love, and the third for fertility.

When attending a Chinese wedding, wear colors that symbolize new life and happiness such yellow, orange, or pink. Avoid black and white, and do not wear red like the bride. *Angbaos* (or red packets) should be given in multiples of twenties rather than tens and ideally the amounts should end with the number 8 (good fortune), such as S $88. Do not give *angbaos* containing the numbers 13 or 4 as these are inauspicious. And ensure the notes are brand new. As to the amount to give, wedding companies recommend taking the cost for your dinner, marking it up by 10 percent, and then rounding it off to ensure an auspicious number. (Locally, the terms *angbao* and *hongbao* are used interchangeably.)

**Malay**

A Malay wedding is equally colorful and elaborate, and usually takes place on Saturday evening and Sunday. Two or three days before the wedding the *berinai* ceremony takes place, in which the bride's palms and feet are decorated with henna dye. On the Saturday the bride waits at her home, which has been elaborately decorated with silk and satin hangings, beaded cushions, and finely embroidered throws. She is the queen of the proceedings, and the groom and his family must wait patiently outside. A *kadi*, an official licensed by the Muslim authorities, speaks to the bride and groom separately, and if they agree to the marriage, they sign the marriage register. The groom then presents the bride with *duit hantaran* or a monetary gift, the amount of which depends on the family's wealth. After this, the solemnization ceremony begins with readings from the *Quran* and the groom taking his oath of marriage and presenting his wife with *mahr* (dowry). *Mahr* is a religious obligation and may be anything from cash to a house; importantly, it can never be taken from her. Although now legally married, the couple do not start living together until after the *bersanding*, or the sitting in state ceremony, which usually takes place the following day.

*Bersanding* is the public celebration of the wedding and is held at the bride's home. In modern Singapore this is usually the landscaped area at the entrance to the HDB estate or the enormous elevator lobby of the block where the girl lives. Marquees for the guests and sumptuously decorated thrones for the bride and groom are hired. The couple reign as King and Queen, with the bride sitting unsmiling and with downcast eyes to symbolize modesty and decorum. The guests sprinkle rose petals and saffron rice on the couple's palms to wish them a fruitful life together, and in return the guests receive chocolate or a cake in a glass, to celebrate fertility. Finally, after the bride and groom step down from their thrones, a traditional banquet is served.

Some couples today will also host their work colleagues at a Western-style reception in a hotel. For this the bride will be dressed in a Western-style wedding dress.

Although Malay weddings are casual affairs, guests should dress appropriately with smart-casual being the order of the day and women in conservative attire. Gifts are not expected but a small sum of money is always appreciated as a blessing, such as S $50 (in 2018, US $36). Ideally, place it in a green packet (red packets are accepted) and give it to one of the couple's parents, or place it in the box provided.

### Indian

The Hindu wedding ceremony traditionally takes hours, but some couples opt for a simpler ceremony. The central rite is when the bride and groom, watched by the priest, walk three times around the sacred fire that represents purity, followed by the groom's tying of the *thali*, a gold chain, around his bride's neck. The *thali* is the equivalent of the Western wedding ring, and this part of the ceremony is noisy, with the ringing of bells and shouts and chants in order to keep evil spirits at bay. Elaborately dressed guests, in saris and adorned with gold jewelry, then throw yellow rice on the newly married couple and give them gifts of either money or jewelry. Even when Indian Christians marry in church, the tying of the *thali* around the bride's neck is an important part of the ceremony.

Indian weddings are colorful and exotic, and smart-casual is a good rule of thumb. Again, it is not compulsory to gift money, but guests generally calculate the cost of the wedding banquet and give this amount. Either drop the packet into the money box or give it to the couple directly.

## FUNERALS
### Chinese
Chinese funerals are highly organized and ritualistic affairs, and the ceremonies can continue for up to seven days until the body is cremated. The first ceremony takes place just after death, when the chief mourner washes the deceased. If the death has occurred in one of the high-rise apartment blocks, the body is taken down by way of the stairs and the embalming and the placing in the coffin is carried out in the open area beneath the apartment block. This is where the mourners gather; sometimes wealthy families hire extra mourners. Food and drink are provided and the mourners sit around and play mah-jong. Loud music is played to keep away evil spirits and also animals, if the gathering is outside.

If in doubt, foreigners should ask colleagues whether it is appropriate to attend the wake. The etiquette at the wake involves filing past the open coffin. You then pay your respects to the bereaved. At this stage Singaporeans generally make a small gift to help with the funeral expenses.

On the day of the funeral the mourners assemble and set off in a cavalcade led by a brightly colored van with the symbol of the tiger, if the deceased was male, or the stork for a woman. In China the tiger is lord of the animals. It represents might and courage, and the white tiger is the guardian of graves. The stork is not only a messenger of the gods, who can carry a person to heaven, but also a symbol of virtue. The procession usually consists of family mourners followed by colorfully dressed musicians. The priest and the hearse follow behind. The bereaved wear sackcloth headbands and straw sandals.

The body is normally cremated, in contrast to the Chinese mainland tradition, reflecting the realities of population density. After the funeral the important ritual of providing the deceased with all the material goods needed in the next life takes place. Traditionally these items were buried with the body, but today houses, cars, and cell phones made of paper are ceremonially burned, after which the funeral party shares a large meal.

### Muslim

When a Muslim dies the Imam is summoned to the house. The body is placed with the head facing Mecca and washed by relatives, after which a white cloth is placed over it. It is the tradition in Islam for the deceased to be buried within twelve hours of death; until then someone stays with the body with the imam reciting prayers. Finally, the body is wrapped in more layers of cloth—the last being seamless—and taken either to the mosque or directly to the graveyard.

### Indian

In the Indian community, when the deceased is a Hindu, the body, after washing, is placed in a wooden coffin with silver coins on the eyes to keep them closed. Two oil lamps are set on either side of the coffin, and the grandchildren process around with lighted candles. The funeral rite is conducted in the home, followed immediately by cremation. As a mark of respect for the dead person, an oil lamp remains burning in the home for as long as forty days after death.

### Burial and Cremation

Land is at a premium in Singapore and burial is no longer a viable option. With Bukit Brown, the oldest Chinese cemetery, being dug up to build a new highway, the traditional Chinese culture of venerating the dead at the graveside is dying out. In fact, most of Singapore's cemeteries have already disappeared and today you can only lease a burial site for fifteen years at the last surviving cemetery, Choa Chu Kang. In contrast, there are three crematoria where ashes can be stored in special wall niches. Even so, the National Environment Agency is offering inland ash scattering as the ecologically preferable option.

## GIFT GIVING

Generally speaking, gifts are given at weddings, Christmas, and Chinese New Year. The main point to remember is its suitability for the occasion. It would be better not to give a gift at all than to give something cheap and tawdry. Don't hand out promotional ballpoint pens or keyrings to negotiating partners! Furthermore, presents should always be wrapped. It would be considered impolite to present an unwrapped gift with the words "I'm sorry I didn't have time to wrap it." In Singapore it is not only the thought that counts, but how the thought is presented. An unwrapped present demonstrates your view of the recipient—he or she is not important enough for the gift to be wrapped. It is worth remembering, not only for Singapore but also for the rest of Asia, that form is of the essence. It is not just what you do that is important, but how you do it.

**Chinese**

The Chinese have many superstitions and you soon learn in Singapore that certain colors, numbers, and everyday items have propitious or inauspicious connotations. Buildings and interiors should be designed according to the principles of Feng Shui—for example, having no sharp edges to ensure harmony.

Red, gold, and pink are the colors associated with good luck and health, fortune and happiness, while white, blue, navy blue, and black are associated with mourning. The "Little Black Dress" won't feature in a traditional Chinese woman's wardrobe, nor the white linen suit associated with life in the tropics for a man.

Similarly, even numbers are looked upon favorably as they are harmonious, while an uneven number signifies loneliness and imbalance. The exceptions to this are 4, 14, and 24, which are unlucky to many Chinese because in Cantonese the number four sounds like the word "dead."

With the exception of Valentine's Day bouquets (when, no doubt, traditional red roses symbolize harmony, love, and good fortune), flowers are not given by the Chinese in Singapore, as they are associated with illness and death. Never send flowers to a new mother; and do not send a card with a stork on it, as a symbolic stork adorns a woman's funeral procession.

A gift of a clock—a favorite retirement gift in the West—would be most inappropriate, as the word "clock" in Cantonese also sounds like "go to a funeral"! Other items to be avoided include handkerchiefs, as they are dispensed at funerals, and sharp objects such as scissors or penknives, which signify the end of a friendship.

When the Chinese give gifts, on occasions such as Chinese New Year or at weddings, they like to give *angbao*—money, preferably brand-new notes, in a red envelope. (See page 73.)

In Singapore, as elsewhere in Asia, it is not the custom to unwrap a gift in front of the giver, but simply to accept it with great pleasure. In this way no embarrassment is felt by either the giver or the receiver when the gift is finally unwrapped.

### Malay

Always remember that they are Muslims—the bottle of brandy that would delight a Chinese colleague would horrify a Malay! Similarly, do not give perfume to a woman if it contains alcohol, and do not give anything made from pigskin. If attending a wedding, a safe present would be something for the kitchen, such as a tea set, kitchen utensils (but not knives), serving dishes, saucepans, and so on. The present can be wrapped in traditional wedding paper or red paper (for love). The giving of money is always appreciated but large amounts are not expected.

Gifts are not usually given to a new mother, but if you wish to do so, a basket of fruit is always appreciated. When visiting the mother at home it is traditional to bring a gift for the baby such as clothing or cuddly toys, but remember, no dogs!

### Indian

Like the Chinese and Malays, the Indians do not open presents in front of the giver. It is good luck to give a sum of money, if appropriate (such as a wedding), in odd numbers; this is best done by adding one dollar to a multiple of ten, for example fifty-one dollars. Avoid beef products or anything made of leather if the recipient is a Hindu, and, though frangipani is considered beautiful and exotic by Westerners, do not gift it or decorate your home with it. It is the flower used in funeral wreaths by the Indian community.

It is common to give a new-born baby gold, such as a bracelet. Baby clothes and soft toys are also welcome and appropriate, but again, no dogs if the family is Muslim.

# chapter four

# THE SINGAPOREANS AT HOME

## SOCIAL AND FAMILY RELATIONSHIPS

Although it is now rare to find all three generations living under the same roof, as would have once been the case in China, India, or Malaysia, the belief in the extended family is still strong. For all three ethnic groups, it is the most important unit in society. It is the means by which religious practice and traditional values are passed down to the next generation, ensuring one's cultural identity is not lost. Consequently, few important decisions are made without the family's approval, whether it concerns the choice of school or university, a likely marriage partner, or business or employment decisions.

In essence, Singapore remains a patriarchal society, even though—from its inception—the constitution declared the equal rights of men and women before the law.

In order to understand the modern Singaporean family, watching the local film *Ilo Ilo* is a must. Directed by Anthony Chen, it was premiered at the 2013 Cannes Film Festival and won the Camera d'Or, the first Singaporean film to do so. Set in 1997 during the Asian financial crisis, it chronicles the life of a middle-class family as they struggle with personal and financial issues.

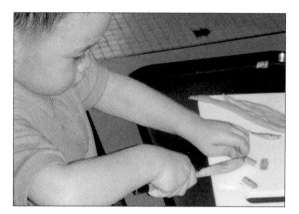

## CHILDREN

Although public displays of affection are frowned upon in Singapore, this does not apply to babies and young children. They are lavished with affection, and often, to Western eyes, overindulged. The real world, with all its triumphs and disappointments, does not begin until a child starts school. Then discipline is strict and physical punishment is acceptable. Caning is legal but its use in the home is being publicly debated.

Great value is placed on education, not only by the parents, who see it as improving their child's future, but also by the state, which considers it the nation's lifeblood. A student is therefore expected to study hard and spend long hours doing homework. Everyone learns English at school, and though Mandarin in the home is replacing the regional dialects of Chinese Singaporean families, many children can still converse in both. In the early years after independence, many Chinese parents campaigned against English being universally taught since, under British rule, their

children were educated in Chinese. Today, however, nobody doubts the wisdom of Lee Kuan Yew's dictate; English has not only been a conduit to economic success, but it serves as a common language in a country that did not have one.

## LIFESTYLE AND HOUSING

While it is true that a handful of very wealthy Singaporeans live in palatial houses on "landed property" (as seen in the film *Crazy Rich Asians*), more than 80 percent live in the high-rise HDB apartments that are available to rent or to buy. These apartments are relatively small and so much of life is lived outdoors—in the open spaces under the buildings, in parks, streets, eating houses, and cafés.

Affluent Singaporeans prefer the luxurious private apartments, complete with swimming pools and squash courts, and price rises in this sector have increased markedly. To avoid a housing bubble, the government has raised taxes on home purchases,

but much of the increase has been caused by foreign buyers purchasing apartments in the popular areas around Orchard Road.

## INVITATIONS HOME

### Gifts

It is always appreciated if a visitor brings a gift, but remember that Malay and Indian Muslims do not drink alcohol and frown upon smoking, so sweets or cakes are safe options. If your hosts are Chinese, remember to keep to even numbers, except 4, 14, and 24, which, as we have seen, are considered unlucky.

### Etiquette

It is a privilege to be invited to a Singaporean home, but it is easy to cause offense inadvertently. In all three communities (and among many Westerners too) it is customary to remove your shoes when entering the home (so wear socks or tights). Remember to dress modestly and always err on the side of being more rather than less formal—no shorts or revealing clothes, even if it is hot and humid outside.

You may be invited to sit on the floor in a Malay home, but since pointing the soles of your feet at a person is considered impolite, men should sit cross-legged, and women should sit sideways with their feet tucked underneath. If you are invited to sit on a sofa or a chair, try not to cross your legs, especially in front of an older person, as this is regarded as rude. Where children are concerned, do not pat the small child or toddler on the head. While this is an act of affection in the West, for a Malay or Indian the head is sacred and should never be touched. Above all, do not use the left hand when eating, shaking hands, or giving gifts in Malay or Indian households, as it is reserved for personal hygiene and considered unclean.

In all three communities it is the tradition to offer some refreshment, however brief the visit, and it would be impolite to refuse. If you are invited to a meal in the evening, remember that Singaporeans tend to rise early and retire early, so take your cue from your hosts. Unlike in the West, guests do not stay on after the meal but leave promptly when it is over. If you are hosting a dinner, do not take it personally!

**Public and Private Areas**
Singaporeans have definite public and private areas, and the visitor can cause grave embarrassment if in conversation he or she unwittingly touches on close personal or family relationships, emotions, romantic attachments, or sexual matters. Displays of affection are frowned upon and the hugging and kissing of

close personal friends of the opposite sex is not done. Discussions about religion or politics are best avoided, and humor does not always travel well—especially British humor, which is often self-deprecating.

## GREETINGS

Chinese people will often shake hands, but it is not the firm, vigorous grip of North America or Northern Europe, but rather a softer, gentler gesture. You may also see an older Chinese man pat a younger friend on the arm as a way of greeting.

When greeting each other, Malays will often "*salaam*," that is, put their palms together and make a small bow. They might use the other traditional Malay greeting of offering both hands to the recipient, lightly touching the person's outstretched hands, then bringing one or two hands back to the heart. Your hosts, knowing you are Western and wanting you to feel at home, may well shake your hand but only if you share the same gender: remember that Malay men and women do not touch the opposite sex. Unlike countries in continental Europe and South America, Singaporeans do not go in for hugging or kissing, even with close friends.

Similarly, in the Indian community different sexes do not shake hands with one another, although an Indian woman will shake hands with another woman and a man with another man. The traditional Indian greeting of *namaste* is similar to the Malay *salaam*.

This is only a guideline, however, and holds very much for the older generation and the religiously devout. Young Singaporeans have adopted Western styles of address, and in international businesses the gentle handshake is the most common form of greeting (see page 144).

## PUBLIC DISPLAY

All ethnic communities respect the wisdom of age and expect dignified behavior to be shown to an older person. It is common for Singaporeans to use the terms Uncle or Auntie for people who are much older than themselves, and it is polite for children to call strangers by these titles. As already mentioned, older Singaporeans may be uncomfortable with touching members of the opposite sex or public displays of affection, so a handshake could be an inappropriate greeting; take your cue from those around you and maintain a reasonable social distance. As we have seen, this is not the case with the younger generation who are less formal and more at ease with Western-style expressions of friendship and affection.

## BOY MEETS GIRL

Dating and courtship within the three communities of Singapore is a relatively new phenomenon and although in the past marriage was considered far too important to be left to casual dating and romance, it is now increasingly common. As elsewhere in the West, young Singaporeans use dating sites and Tinder, and discuss on social media whether the man should foot the first-date bill or whether going-dutch is acceptable. Multiple dates might still be frowned on by some, but casual sex is more common than admitted in public. Of course, parents tend to disapprove of such behavior, and dating below the age of seventeen is discouraged as children should spend their time studying.

Nonetheless, arranged marriages still exist among the Malay and Indian communities, where finding a partner from a similar background and complementary personality is best left to parents who understand their offspring. Chinese and Indian families will check the respective horoscopes and some Indian families may still consider caste.

Interracial marriage has increased from 15 percent in 2006 to 21.5 percent in 2017. The most likely reason is the multiracial nature of post-secondary education and the workplace. However, there is a difference in preference. Chinese families prefer their children to date Caucasians, whereas Malay and Indian families favor the Chinese. At the same time, researchers point out the tendency for Singaporeans not to share their cultural practices and hence those of Chinese descent do not always appreciate, for example, the importance of Malay practices such as *halal* food, the headscarf, and taboos against alcohol and touching dogs.

When visiting Singapore it is important to remember these different cultural expectations and to take things slowly. Most Singaporean women still consider a sexual relation to indicate serious intent.

## NATIONAL SERVICE

At the age of sixteen-and-a-half every Singaporean male has to register for two years' national service (NS) and later reserve duty until the age of forty. A deferment for full-time studies can be acquired pending completion of their studies, but any attempt to evade NS can result in three-year imprisonment and/or a hefty fine. The government considers it essential to building strength of character and developing leadership skills. At the same time, it is an ideal opportunity for the different strands of society to mix together and forge a sense of national pride.

## NAMES

In Singapore the three ethnic groups refer to themselves in different ways, and though the society is becoming ever more informal it is advisable to master the correct use of personal names and titles. This can be complicated, however, so if in doubt, seek local advice.

Generally, when making introductions and in formal meetings it is advisable to use a person's title first and then their family or personal name, for example "President Lee." Titles are usually reserved for superiors, not equals or juniors. Although many younger Singaporeans adopt a Western-style personal name, such as Lucy or Brian Wong, for everyday use, most older Singaporeans do not, and it is always better to err on the side of formality rather than risk causing offense.

**Chinese**
Chinese conventions can be fraught with difficulty for the Western visitor, and something of a revelation when you work out the system.

Given the importance of family to the Chinese, the family name is always given precedence. For example, if a man's family name is Wong, he will be called "Mr. Wong." Mr. Wong probably has two given names, so he might be Wong Chok Yew. This is where it gets complicated, because the name Chok will have been given to all the sons of that generation in the family. Finally, he will have his personal name, Yew. Therefore Mr. Wong's full name is presented, from the general to the particular, as Wong Chok Yew.

In formal situations, it is a good idea to address somebody as Mr., Miss, or Madam, followed by the family name, for example "Miss Lee." Friends will call each other by their given names but in a business situation take your cue from your counterpart.

Traditionally, Chinese women retain their own (paternal) family name on marriage since they are not of their husband's bloodline. Hence, even if Mr. Wong's wife is known by her Western friends as Mrs. Wong, this is not, technically, her name. If her maiden name was Lee Bee Wah (Lee being the paternal family name), she becomes Mrs. Lee. Sometimes Chinese women change their name by joining it with that of their husband—in this case she may be Mrs. Lee-Wong Bee Wah. Occasionally the honorific title of Madam is used, as in Madam Mao Tse Tung or Madam Chang Kai Shek.

In Singapore, Chinese women tend to use their husband's name. If they want to retain their own name, they use their maiden name plus "Madam." Like the men, they will often adopt a Western personal name, especially if working for a foreign company, so Lee Bee Wah might refer to herself as "Betty."

If this seems complicated, just ask. Remember, Chinese people are equally bemused by Western names, especially if a person's name is Robert and suddenly they hear him being referred to as Bob, or Alexandra as Sandra. Tell them how you wish to be called from the beginning to avoid awkward situations.

The honorific terms of Auntie and Uncle are used to refer to someone much older than yourself, and children always refer to older people who are not their relatives in this way.

**Malay**
Malay men attach their father's name to the end of their own name and use the word *bin*, which means "son of." So, for example, Ali bin Osman is Ali, son of Osman.

Similarly, women use *binti*, or "daughter of." So, Fatima binti Osman is Fatima, daughter of Osman. Her friends will call her Fatima and in more formal terms she will be addressed as *Puan* (Mrs.) Fatima or Mrs. Fatima. As with the Chinese and Indian communities, some Malay married women (especially those in business) will adopt their husband's name in the Western manner. If you see the word *Hajji* or the feminine *Hajjiah* in a person's name, it means that he or she has undertaken the pilgrimage to Mecca.

## Indian

The forebears of the majority of the Indians in Singapore came from Tamil Nadu, where they do not use family names. Instead they use the initial of their father's name placed before their own personal name. For example, a woman named Radhika would call herself M. Radhika, where M is the first letter of the name of her father, Murugesan. After marriage, Radhika will be addressed as Mrs. Radhika, followed by her husband's personal name or both his names.

Not all Indians in Singapore are Hindu or Muslim—some are Sikh and others Christian. Unlike the Chinese, if you hear an Indian refer to himself by his Christian name, such as Thomas or Patrick, then he will be a Christian, and has not adopted a Western name for ease of pronunciation.

Most Sikhs have three names: a personal name, a name to show Sikh identity ("Singh," or "lion," for a male), and a clan or sub-sect name. Many Sikh names are the same as, or similar to, Hindu ones. All Sikhs are Singhs, but not all Singhs are Sikhs. (Singh, meaning lion, is included in the name of Singapore!) Men are often addressed as "Sardarji" (abbreviated to S.), which is an honorific similar to "Mr." Most personal names can be used for both males and females. Women often just use "Kaur" (meaning "princess") as a third name, but can also use "Singh," as many families have taken this as a surname.

# chapter five

# FOOD & DRINK

## COOKING STYLES

Food plays an important role in the social life of Singaporeans. Eating is considered a national pastime and part of the national identity, and food is, quite literally, an obsession. The blending and adapting of the Chinese, Malay, and Indian culinary traditions has resulted in a distinctive gastronomy that blends the modern and the traditional. For a foodie, this country is a delight. There is everything from local eateries to Michelin-star restaurants. Bijou coffee houses brush up against global fast-food chains, and pizzas are as popular with the young as Hainanese chicken rice.

Typical Singaporean food can be divided into five categories—rice, noodles, seafood, meat, and snacks (or desserts)—and is promoted as an attraction by the tourist board. Every July the Singapore Food Festival celebrates the varied cuisine. Famous chefs such as Anthony Bourdain and Gordon Ramsay have hailed the hawker food tradition and have popularized some of its dishes on their television shows.

When considering seafood, chilli crab and black pepper crab are quintessential and must be sampled, whereas Hainanese chicken rice is probably one of the country's most popular dishes. *Satay* made with pork, chicken, or beef is a common snack and found in most food courts, while fried *Hokkien mee* is a standard noodle dish made with prawns and sliced pork. Another popular noodle meal is a soup made from coconut prawn broth called *Nyonya laksa*. Despite the Cantonese community being relatively small, *dim sum* is found in most local eateries as well as upmarket restaurants and is considered by many to be the ultimate comfort food. Note that it is served from the morning to the afternoon and seldom at dinner, so look out for the *dim sum* hours.

Singaporeans tend to eat three main meals a day. *Kaya* toast (toasted white bread with butter and sweet coconut jam) is a popular breakfast with coffee and condensed milk. The Indian *Roti prata* (see page 98) is also common. Rice or noodles are eaten at lunch, often in a food court, and supper can be quite late.

## Chinese

The best place to experience Chinese food is at the large banquets where guests sit around a circular

table and sample eight to nine dishes (see page 106). Crystal Jade is a chain of Singaporean restaurants with a Michelin star rating and numerous Michelin Bib Gourmand awards. Offering modern interpretations of traditional food, they are popular among the locals. You can eat alone or in a large group, and takeaway options are available.

During Chinese New Year, try to experience the Prosperity Toss known as *Lo Hei* or *Yusheng*. With its roots in southern China, the Singaporean version is made of shredded white and green radish (representing prosperity at work and eternal youth respectively), carrots (good luck), ginger and onion slices, pomelo, peanut dust (a home filled with gold), and so on. Guests gather around the dish and toss the shredded ingredients into the air with their chopsticks shouting "*lo hei.*" The higher the toss, the greater the fortune!

### Peranakan

Peranakan cuisine—developed by the early Chinese immigrants who settled in Malacca, Penang, and

later Singapore—is particularly interesting. Key ingredients are coconut milk, galangal, tamarind juice, candlenuts, torch ginger bud, and kaffir lime leaf. The Singaporean Peranakans are more heavily influenced by Indonesian traditions, and *laksa lemak* is common. Recipes are handed down from generation to generation and in the past a daughter-in-law was judged by the quality of her cooking.

There are a number of quality Peranakan restaurants that merit a visit, such as True Blue, located near the Peranakan Museum in Armenian Street. Decked in the style of a Peranakan home, you receive the full Nyonya experience; ask the waiter for advice as to what to eat but specialities include *otak-otak* (fish, spices, and coconut milk wrapped in banana leaf) and *ayam buak keluak*, a unique dish made with chicken and nuts from the kepayang tree. In 2018 Violet Oon was the grande dame of Singaporean food and an ambassador for Peranakan cuisine, with restaurants in Bukit Timah, the National Gallery, and Clarke Quay.

## Malay

Popular Malay foods include the ubiquitous curry puff (flaky pastry filled with curried chicken, potato, and a hard-boiled egg) and *mee goreng* and *nasi goreng*, the former made of yellow wheat noodles and the latter of rice. *Nasi lemak* is made of rice cooked in coconut milk and pandan leafs and served with sambal, anchovies, and other condiments such as peanuts and vegetables. *Soto ayam*, a spicy chicken soup, is also a staple of the food courts, as is the famous *rendang* made with beef, spices, and coconut milk.

### Indian

In Little India, most eateries will serve *roti prata*, a fried bread pancake that is served with egg, curry, or sugar or any possible variation, including ice cream. *Dosa* is a common rice and lentil pancake, and the hearty North Indian mutton soup, or *Kambing*, is found in most food courts. *Murtabak*, a classic Indian Muslim dish consisting of bread stuffed with minced meat and onion, is also popular.

### Western

There are many top restaurants and international chefs, and everything from French *haute cuisine* to New York-style burgers can be enjoyed. Western influence has also made its way into the food court culture, where "chicken chops" with mushroom sauce are served with mashed potato.

## DIETARY RESTRICTIONS
### Chinese

Apart from Buddhists in the south of China who shun beef, the Chinese have no restrictions on what they can or cannot eat. Indeed, the Chinese greeting is not "Hello" or "How are you?" but "Have you eaten?" The reply, incidentally, is always "Yes," even if you haven't.

This does not mean to say that all Singaporean Chinese like the same food: those who come from northern China prize mutton and lamb while those from the south heartily dislike it. However, just as dark chicken meat is considered a delicacy by all

Singaporeans, rice and noodles are equally popular. It is fair to say, however, that large slabs of meat, such as rare steak, are avoided by most.

Although the Chinese love to eat, they eat with health very much in mind. They believe that certain foods are "Yin," or "cooling." Foods such as pork, watermelon, and apples cool the body and are good in summer. "Yang" foods on the other hand are considered to be hearty, such as fried foods, chocolate, and lychees. The ideal is to balance the Yin and Yang in a meal and to eat in moderation.

## Malay

For a Muslim, certain foods are *halal* (permitted) and some are *haram* (forbidden). Pork is *haram* and must never be consumed; all other meats must be slaughtered according to Islamic law if they are to be considered *halal*. Alcohol is also forbidden, as is any food containing blood. It is now possible to find Chinese restaurants cooking *halal* food in the Kampong Glam area.

## Indian

Devout Hindus will tend to follow a lacto-vegetarian diet, that is, they will avoid meat, poultry, fish, and eggs, but will eat milk products such as a yogurt. Beef is prohibited as the cow is sacred, and priests require certain people to prepare their food for them. Ayurvedic medicine shares similar beliefs with the Chinese: to be healthy, a person must eat specific "hot" or "cold" producing foods to rectify any imbalance in the body.

## FOOD COURTS

Hawkers once roamed the streets of Singapore selling all kinds of tasty foods. Now they have been relocated to food courts, permanent centers that have become an integral part of Singapore life. These can be found everywhere, from backstreets to air-conditioned shopping malls. Clean and affordable, they are bustling, noisy places, full of smells coming from steaming pots and sizzling pans, with orders being shouted to the cooks. You can find everything from local favorites to Italian pasta. Many people regularly eat at such venues and all have their favorite places; it is common to arrive at a food court and see a long line outside a particular stall while others are empty.

They represent excellent value for money and there are those who swear that the meals in such places are just as good as, if not better than, meals served in many upscale restaurants. In fact, Michelin awarded two such stalls a star each for their culinary expertise, and the government plans to build twenty more centers in the next decade. Newton Food Court is probably the most famous and many tourists will flock there for the fish, but it is worth walking down to your local center and eating with the regulars.

One aspect of hawker etiquette to note is "chopping," that is, the habit of putting a packet of tissues on a table to reserve it. Do not remove them and sit down, but by all means place your own while you go off to browse the different stalls.

### KOPITIAMS

The word "*kopitiam*" is an amalgamation of the Malay for coffee (*kopi*) and the Hokkien for shop (*tiam*). More than a coffee shop, it is also a place to meet friends and eat. Here you can sample the *kopi* that is taken with condensed milk and *kaya* toast.

## CZE CHAS

Meaning "eating house," these open-air eateries are found everywhere. They offer table service and more extensive menus than the food courts, and a good place to start is Chinatown where some establishments specialize in just one dish.

## DRINK

Two popular local drinks are *kopi* (or coffee, served sweet with condensed milk) and bubble tea, which is a sweet milk tea mixed with chewy pearls. You will also come across *bandung* (an ice-cold drink made with milk and rose cordial) and sugar cane-juice. *Teh tarik* is famous for the way the Indian tea-makers pour it from one vessel to another (known as "stretching") and serve it hot and frothy. Generally, most Westerners find Singaporean drinks too sweet for their palate, so feel free to ask for "less sugar" or no "sugar."

Chinese tea is the normal accompaniment to any Chinese meal. They believe it prevents obesity by washing away the fats ingested with the food, and when taken after a meal it helps digestion. Often they will drink one or two glasses before a banquet where alcoholic toasts are to be given. They tend not to take coffee after meals.

As a general rule, the Chinese do not like drinking without eating, and therefore dislike cocktail parties. They will drink beer with their meal, usually the local Singapore brew "Tiger Beer," and, surprisingly, given their dislike of iced drinks, they drink it cold. They also like drinking brandy and whiskey—the more expensive the better, as it is seen as a status symbol.

For Indian and Malay Muslims alcohol is strictly forbidden but this does not mean that the less devout are abstinent; many enjoy the city's growing wine and cocktail culture. However, the high alcohol levy makes a night out on the town expensive. It was not uncommon, in 2017, to pay S $10 (US $7 in 2018) for a pint of Tiger beer at a hawker stall and S $35 (US $25 in 2018) for a Singapore Sling—Singapore's most celebrated cocktail—at the legendary Long Bar of Raffles Hotel.

## SINGAPORE SLING

### ORIGINAL RECIPE
2 parts Gin
1 part Cherry Brandy
1 part Benedictine
1 part Triple Sec
2 parts Pineapple Juice
2 parts Orange Juice
1 part Lime Juice

### QUICK AND SIMPLE RECIPE
3 parts Gin
1 part Cherry Brandy
Juice of 1 Lemon

In both recipes mix and strain into a tall glass,
top with soda water, and decorate with sliced orange,
lemon or lime, and a cherry.

## BANQUETS AND ENTERTAINING

All business as well as most social entertaining is done
in restaurants. These are usually dinners, but can be
lunches as well. Banquets are a feature of Chinese
business life and the celebration of major family
events. The banquet will usually take place in a
private dining room in a hotel or restaurant and, as
Singapore is a hierarchical society, guests may arrive
in order of rank.

### Eating Etiquette

Eating is a communal event in all ethnic groups,
although the manner of dining differs. For the Malays,
Indians, and Straits Chinese, eating with your fingers
is the only true way to enjoy curry, but spoons are
always provided, and you will not find any Singaporean
eating without cutlery at a smart restaurant. When
eating with your hand, only the right is used because,
among traditional Hindus and Muslims, the left hand
is reserved for personal hygiene. Even then only the
tips of the fingers of the right hand are used, and it is
considered most impolite to touch another person's
food with your fingers. When helping yourself from a
communal dish always use the serving spoon provided.
Diners wash their hands before the meal, and you
may find yourself being offered a bowl of warm water
and a napkin both before and after a meal in finer
Indian or Malay restaurants. Even in the most basic of
establishments you will often see a row of washbasins
provided for the use of customers.

For the Chinese, dining etiquette is somewhat
different as the use of chopsticks is the norm. However,
you can always ask for a fork and spoon without shame,

and many restaurants and hawkers will provide both. There are certain straightforward rules governing their use. For instance, never put your chopsticks upright in a bowl of rice as it symbolizes death. It is also considered bad manners to wave your chopsticks about, point them at somebody, or make a noise with them (although it is more than acceptable to drink soup noisily or slurp noodles). It is permissible, from time to time, to rest one's chopsticks on the rest stand, never across the dinner plate or rice bowl. It is bad manners to reach across another person's chopsticks in order to get at the food on display.

Unlike in the West, guests do not stay long chatting and drinking coffee after the end of the meal. When everyone has finished eating, that is the end of the festivities and generally all the guests leave at the same time.

For the Malays, forks and spoons will usually be provided for a meal, but not knives as these are considered to be weapons. However, don't worry as any meat will already have been cut up into bite-sized portions. The fork is held in the left hand and used to push the food on to the spoon. It is considered impolite to make a noise with a spoon when serving yourself, and you should always ask your host to join you in eating. The Malays are delighted if you take second helpings and, unlike the Chinese, do not think you are being greedy, so you do not have to protest when offered more, but graciously accept. On the other hand, it is considered rude to refuse food, so at least try to sample a small piece when served. If you absolutely cannot eat the food proffered you should invent a good excuse, such as an allergy.

**Seating Arrangements**

Typically, the table will be round with a revolving central platform for the dishes, so the whole group can see, speak to each other, and help themselves to food without interruption. The place of honor, unlike in the West, is on the left side of the host. The more junior guests sit with their backs to the front entrance. This comes from the time when it was feared that armed assailants could burst into a room and attack those nearest the door first. However relaxed the evening is there will always be a seating plan, and so one waits to be seated. Of course, the host does not take his seat until everyone else has taken theirs.

So as not to be seen to be bragging about the evening's fare, the host will probably say a few words about the paucity and insignificance of the food on offer. The guests respond to this humble stance by admiring the food as it appears, and discussing with fellow guests the subtle flavoring and composition of each dish. Usually a banquet consists of eight or ten courses and the dishes appear one at a time. The use of chopsticks is *de rigueur* at an event like this, but at home many Chinese use forks, spoons, and plates.

## Making Speeches and Proposing Toasts
In order not to spoil the enjoyment of the food, all speeches are made before the banquet begins. To commence the proceedings the host will raise his glass and propose a toast, or simply say *"Ch'ing."* The other guests similarly raise their glasses, holding the glass in both hands, the fingers of the right hand under its bottom, the left hand holding it. There can be further toasts throughout the meal when each new course appears.

It is a good idea to pace yourself at a banquet, or you risk being overwhelmed by the time the last dish appears. You are not obliged to eat a lot of any food you do not like, but you should eat whatever you serve yourself. Always take the food from the dish nearest to you on the revolving circular table top.

## Reciprocating
It is part of doing business in Singapore to be entertained and to entertain in return, and even though your own country may be far less formal, Singaporeans will usually feel more comfortable if entertained "Singapore style." Whether the "return match" is in your own country or in Singapore, the same basic rules apply.

First, the hotel or restaurant chosen should be of sufficiently high standing and reputation to impress your guests. Second, the function will need to be held in a private dining room. When considering the menu, it is a good idea to establish whether any of your guests are Singaporean Malays or Indians as the menu will need to reflect this. Muslims do not eat pork or drink alcohol and Indians are often vegetarian.

If you are entertaining in Singapore seek local advice as to the suitability of the venue, the menu, and the number of courses that would be appropriate. It is important to get help with the seating plan—and name place cards, with correct spellings and title, of course—in this hierarchical society. The Western practice of "sit anywhere" causes great confusion and embarrassment. You as the host will need to be there in plenty of time, not only to greet your guests but also to check that everything is in order.

Arranging this in your home territory might prove a little more difficult. It is always sensible to play it safe and entertain in a Chinese restaurant, albeit one of excellent standing. Singaporeans will feel at home in such a place, and if any of the team is Malay or Indian, the restaurant will be able to provide suitable vegetarian dishes. Chinese restaurants in the West are, of course, familiar with private dining rooms, and will nearly always have one or be prepared to screen off part of the restaurant for the visiting party. You might wish to dine in the chosen restaurant beforehand to see if it and the service are up to the mark, and then spend some time talking to the management about your requirements for the meal. A careful and methodical approach pays handsome dividends as your guests will realize that you have gone to a lot of trouble on their behalf and will be suitably impressed.

### *HOW NOT TO DO IT*

The senior managers of a Western company inadvertently entertained their Singaporean colleagues in the worst possible way. The hosts chose a very prestigious hotel with a splendid private dining room, but after this things went from bad to worse.

First, they had drinks before dinner, not realizing that Singaporeans feel distinctly unhappy drinking without food, and do not like to eat too late either.

The menu was chosen with care, but with no thought as to the requirements of their guests. The main course was rare roast beef. Singaporean Chinese do not like eating large pieces of meat, let alone eating it rare, and as for the Malays and Indians, it was a disaster.

Dessert followed in the same vein. Singaporeans always have fresh fruit sliced into small portions, but on this occasion a large chocolate pudding was served. This was far too rich for the guests, and as for the cheese course that followed, Singaporeans as a rule dislike dairy products.

The meal finished with coffee, and each guest was given a present of an unwrapped ballpoint pen with the logo of the host company.

The entire occasion was an example of how not to entertain Singaporeans. Fortunately, despite the *faux pas*, the business relationship did not founder, and eventually, after a more appropriate meal, a deal beneficial to both parties was signed!

# chapter six

# TIME OUT

## TOURISM

For six years in a row, Changi airport has been rated the best in the world. With its rooftop pool and orchid-filled gardens, its movie theater and art installation, its gourmet restaurants and luxury stores, it is worth the jet lag most intercontinental travelers will suffer to arrive here. It illustrates continued government investment in the tourist industry and, as a consequence, Singapore's meteoric rise as a favored holiday destination. With its reputation for being safe and clean, it offers traditional cultures, cutting-edge architecture, nightlife, shopping, and food, and continues to attract millions of visitors each year. In fact, tourism contributes 10.2 percent of Singapore's GDP, and this is forecast to rise to 14 percent in the near future.

## DESTINATIONS

### Chinatown

Sir Stamford Raffles allocated an area south of the Singapore River for the first Chinese immigrants arriving in 1819. Soon thousands joined them, largely from the central and southern Chinese coastal provinces, and Chinatown became a lively trading

settlement. This it remained until the 1970s, when the government started to replace the old buildings with modern HDB apartments. Belatedly it was realized that this threatened the loss of yet another atmospheric part of old Singapore, and the city architects began a program of renovation and restoration.

Today, Chinatown is a dynamic and bustling mix of old and new, where you can find shophouses

selling traditional medicines next to fashionable bars and lifestyle shops. Here you get a feeling of what Singapore must have been like in the early 1900s, streets thronged with people and filled with the sound of different dialects. Pagoda Street is famous for its stalls where you can buy an array of Chinese-imported trinkets as well as more expensive lacquer ware. Many of the oldest temples are located here,

such as the Sri Mariamman Temple, built by Hindu immigrants in 1827, as well the modern Buddhist Temple of the Tooth. Foodies will love the street, which is lined with stalls and eateries, while those interested in history can enter the world of the coolies in the Chinatown Heritage Centre.

The best way to explore Chinatown is on foot, giving yourself at least three or four hours as there is a lot to see. Remember, the weather is hot and humid and can be debilitating if you are not used to it.

**Kampong Glam, or Arab Street**

The area north of the Singapore River and west of the Rochor River was designated a Muslim settlement by Raffles and soon attracted Arab traders. Today it still reflects the traditions of those Arab seafarers, Indonesians, and Malays who came to settle here. The shops are a blaze of color, selling cloth of all kinds, including silks and batik, rugs, brassware, gold, and

jewelry, as well as rattan ware and basketry that overflow onto the sidewalk. The air is filled with marvelous smells coming from the many *halal* restaurants, especially around the Sultan Mosque. Haji Lane, once a back street, is now bustling with quirky boutiques and cafés, while the grounds of the Istana ("palace" in Malay) house the Malay Heritage Centre.

The island's first mosque was built in 1826, thanks to a generous grant from the East India Company, and replaced a hundred years later with the Sultan Mosque. It is now the city's principal mosque, with a golden dome, towers, and minarets, and can accommodate five thousand worshipers. Visits are strictly regulated, but the best time to go is during the month of Ramadan when the sun sets and the faithful throng the streets and break their fast at the numerous eating houses.

Kampong Glam applies not only to Arab Street but to the whole area bounded by Rochor Canal Road, Jalan Sultan, Victoria Street, and Beach Road. The easiest way to get there is to take the MRT to Bugis, or to go by taxi.

### Little India
Unlike Chinatown or Kampong Glam, Little India was not designated as an ethnic quarter, but grew of its own volition in the latter half of the nineteenth century. It is largely concentrated north of the Rochor Canal and is easy to get to—simply take the MRT and alight at Little India station. The main artery, Serangoon Road, stretches a mile from Rochor Canal Road to Lavender Street, and can be explored on foot. It is one of the most vibrant quarters with its mix of Hindu and Chinese temples, mosques, and churches.

There is so much to see, delicious foods to smell and sample, and wonderful items to buy.

The Little India Arcade, a cluster of shops from the colonial era, is filled with flower-garland sellers, boutique stalls, and exquisite sari fabrics, as well as goldsmiths selling jewelry created from ancient Indian patterns. The open-air Tekka Centre is a noisy, sensory delight where you can watch brewers "pull" the hot milk tea and marvel at the fish counters and spice stalls. Don't forget to go upstairs where you will find row upon row of dazzling saris, shoes, and tailors. A famous 24-hour shopping experience is the Mustafa Centre, composed of two buildings linked by a bridge. Here the merchandise is piled high and you have to squeeze through rows of everything from groceries to electronics.

All this can easily take a good half day, and Sundays are best avoided unless you like crowds. It is the day when migrant workers come to chat, eat, worship, and shop. However, during Deepavali (around October or November) the crowds are part of the colorful and magnificent spectacle, and you can join the devotees as the Silver Chariot is processed along the road.

**Historic Singapore and the Civic Center**

At the heart of the old colonial settlement is the Padang ("field" in Malay), a large, well-tended open space surrounded by trees that was earmarked by Raffles as a recreation ground soon after his arrival. Here are the grand colonial buildings that once formed the civic center of the city and have now been restored, with Parliament House forming the new Arts Centre, and City Hall and the Supreme Court housing the National Gallery. The Asian Civilisation Museum with its neo-classical architecture is worth a visit, as are the Victoria Theatre and Concert Hall. Nearby is Esplanade Park and the Theatres on the Bay, locally known as "the Durian" because its curved dome resembles the fruit. Nearby you will notice the Chopsticks, standing 220 feet (67 meters) tall. These four pillars (representing two pairs of chopsticks) symbolize the four peoples of Singapore and is a memorial to the civilians killed during the Japanese Occupation.

Many of the great civic buildings were designed by the Irish architect George Coleman, whose gravestone can be found at Fort Canning, together with those of other early settlers. It is a sobering to realize how many of the first British arrivals died in their twenties of tropical diseases. The hill itself, in addition to containing the ruins of the fort, is landscaped with shrubs and trees and has views over the city.

**Marina Bay**

Edging the former civic center is this iconic and dazzling reclamation site that was begun in 1969 and completed in 2008. Some of the most spectacular views of the city can be had from Sands SkyPark and

Marina Bay Sands, designed by the famous architect Moshe Safdie. The skyline is impressive, while the waterfront promenade is filled with alfresco bars, sculptures, and kite flyers. For those interested in the arts, the lotus-shaped ArtScience Museum hosts exhibitions from around the world, while nearby is the futuristic and vast "Gardens by the Bay," with its conservatories and world-famous Supertrees.

### Singapore Quays

The three main quays along the Singapore River—Boat Quay, Clarke Quay, and Roberston Quay—were once the commercial hub of the city. When the ships moved to ports outside the city in the 1960s, however, the area was abandoned and fell into decline. The clean-up river campaign began in the 1980s and the old shophouses of Boat Quay were declared a conservation zone. Today the area is known for its cafés and bars where shophouses nestle below soaring skyscrapers and boats take tourists up and down the river. Clarke Quay is the buzzing center with its nightclubs and floating junks transformed into restaurants, while Robertson Quay, a little to the west, is more relaxed and tranquil.

### Raffles Hotel

A visit to Singapore would not be complete without a visit to the legendary Raffles Hotel. Since opening its doors in 1887 it has epitomized colonial elegance, luxury, and style, and given rise to the exotic Singapore Sling cocktail. Writers such as Joseph Conrad, Rudyard Kipling, and Somerset Maugham stayed here, as did movie stars like Ava Gardner and Elizabeth Taylor.

### Joo Chiat, or Katong

If you are interested in Peranakan culture, then it is worth taking a bus or taxi to Katong district. This area of prewar architecture and colorful shophouses is a popular eating destination for many Singaporeans. Here Peranakan culture and food can still be enjoyed, and Peranakan handicrafts are also on sale. The East Coast beach is also within walking distance.

### Tiong Bahru

One of the trendiest places in Singapore today, Tiong Bahru is a quaint, local community and the oldest housing estate in the country. Once a burial ground, it is known for its 1930s architecture and famous cafés. Here you will find independent bookshops, vintage LP shops, and lifestyle boutiques.

### Dempsey Hill

This lesser known but fascinating huddle of shopping and eating houses was formerly a nutmeg plantation in the 1850s and then a military camp known as Tanglin Barracks. Redeveloped in 2007, it is now a lifestyle destination close to the Botanic Gardens. From here, you can stroll along its trails and spy on the famous black-and-white houses that were once home to the British colonialists and are now popular among the wealthier European expats.

## Orchard

This is the shopaholic center of Singapore. Named after the nutmeg orchards that grew here in colonial times, it is also the residential zone of Singapore's elite. Most of the old buildings have gone and have been replaced with 1.37 miles (2.2 km) of air-conditioned malls. There are fifteen five-star hotels, four multiscreen cineplexes, about twenty-five malls, and innumerable places to eat. This is not the place to shop if you are looking for a bargain!

Famous stores include Tangs, which sits on a corner site opposite Orchard MRT station, with its Chinese-style green roof and red pillars. An example of a Chinese rags-to-riches story, it was built more than sixty years ago by a former lace peddler, C. K. Tang, who had the foresight to see that Orchard Road would become a bustling thoroughfare. He subsequently brought building materials from his home in Swatow province in China and started constructing a department store.

In 1982 the site was redeveloped and now contains not only a department store but also a high-rise hotel. Today it is a leading home-grown department store selling the best of local fashion and design.

## Gardens

For those interested in horticulture or in search of a few peaceful hours, a trip to the Botanical Gardens, Gardens by the Bay, or Chinese Garden to the west of the city is worthwhile. They are all close to MRT stations and easy to get to (Botanic Gardens, Bayfront, and Chinese Garden respectively).

## Sentosa

This tiny island, immediately south of Singapore, was formerly a British military base. It is now a favorite resort for locals and tourists alike. The main attractions are the Resorts World, which includes the Universal Studios theme park, and the Marine Life Park. There is also the Maritime Experiential Museum and, at night, the Lake of Dreams water, fire, and light display. On offer, too, is a round of golf or a flutter at the casino, and a retreat spa for those who wish to relax.

If you fancy being a little less active, a visit to the southwestern coast of the island will take you to sparkling beaches created from specially imported sand, coconut palms, and flowering shrubs.

You can take the monorail from Vivocity or the cable car from Habourfront.

### Pulau Ubin Islands

For the more adventurous, there is St. John's Island, just under four miles (6 km) south of Singapore, which is less developed than Sentosa. Formerly a quarantine station for cholera cases in the nineteenth century, it is also the site of Raffles' anchorage before he met the Malay chief of Singapore in 1819. There are no hotels here, but you can book a bungalow to rent, and take a trip to neighboring Kusu island. Remember to bring food and water as there are no shops. You can swim in the peaceful lagoons, picnic in certain designated spots, and watch a wide variety of bird life, some of which has made a successful bid for freedom from the bird sellers on the main island. It is about a twenty-minute boat ride from Marina South Pier. Check with your hotel for the times of sailings.

To step back in time and see the Singapore of seventy years ago, visit the island of Pulau Ubin, about one and a half miles (2 km) off the northeastern corner of Singapore, home to the last real *kampong* and fewer than a hundred villagers. Here you can admire the traditional Malay stilt fishing huts or visit one of the Taoist or Buddhist temples. The more energetic can rent mountain bikes to explore the forests and mangrove swamps that abound with wildlife. Details of these activities can be obtained from the visitor center near the ferry. Bumboats leave from Changi Point once there are enough people on board. As there are no ATMS on the island, be sure to bring enough cash.

## Indonesia
Regular ferry services also operate between Singapore and the nearby Indonesian islands of Batam and Bintan. Go online for information and offers.

### MONEY
The local currency is Singapore dollars and cents. US dollars and British pounds are sometimes accepted in major shopping centers and big department stores, but the exchange rate is poor. There is no restriction on the amount of currency you can bring into the country, but amounts over S $20,000 should be declared (US $14,560 in 2018). Credit cards are accepted and surcharges on these are not permitted.

Banking hours are Monday to Friday, 10:00 a.m. to 3:00 p.m., and Saturday, 9:30 a.m. to 1:00 p.m. (some banks are open until 3:00 p.m. and some not at all). Banks in Orchard Road may be open on Sunday from 9:30 a.m. to 3:00 p.m. ATMS are located all over the city and most allow VISA and Mastercard withdrawals.

Most banks change foreign currency. Passports are required and a commission may be charged. Apart from banks and hotels, money can be changed wherever the sign "licensed money changer" is displayed, which applies to most shopping complexes. Visitors are discouraged from changing money with unlicensed money changers.

---

### *TIPPING*

Tipping is not expected in Singapore and certainly not encouraged. Taxi drivers will never round up the bill, so it is up to you whether you wish to do so or not. Note that most hotels and restaurants have a 10 percent service charge, and "++" following a menu price means that the 7 percent Goods and Services Tax (GST) and 10 percent service charge are not included.

---

## SHOPPING

Of course, no visit to Singapore would be complete without a shopping trip or two, or three, and one of these expeditions must include Orchard Road, the legendary street whose name derives from the many nutmeg and pepper plantations that lined the streets until the early years of the twentieth century, when a mysterious disease wiped them out. How very different it looks today: here you will be spoiled for choice. Large department stores, shopping malls, and exclusive boutiques offer a range of international products as well as Asian artifacts, furniture, Persian carpets, jewelry, table linen, silks, batiks, and the latest electronic goods. Despite the heat and humidity, you can shop in comfort as the malls and shops are air-conditioned and many of them are interlinked.

However, if you are interested in bargains and lower prices in general, take the MRT to one of the suburbs and experience shopping like the locals. Nearly every housing estate has its shopping center with a variety of shops, from the humble corner store to elegant designer label shops. Shops are usually open from 10:00 a.m. until 9:00 or 10:00 p.m., and are open on public holidays as well.

For those interested in antiques, a visit to Just Anthony in Paya Leber Road is an experience, with its warehouse-style collection of antique furniture, reproductions, and curios. Or wander along Dempsey Road where you can browse in shops such as Woody Antique House and Shang Antiques and then stop off for a snack at one of the many bars and restaurants.

Around November each year at the F1 Pit Building, the Affordable Art Fair hosts more than sixty-five exhibitors, showcasing contemporary art from all over the world. Artworks range from ink paintings in the traditional style to sculpture and photography.

### The Great Singapore Sale

This month-long event takes place in June or July, in the run-up to National Day. It is organized by the Singapore Retailers Association; some shops offer discounts of up to 70 percent and the leading department stores such as Robinsons and Tangs are worth a visit. However, don't forget to visit Chinatown, Kampong Glam, and Little India where small independent shops also participate in the event.

### Sales Tax

Most shops levy a 7 percent Goods and Services Tax (GST), but you are eligible for a refund when you leave if your purchases exceed S $100 (US $73 in 2018) and the shop has completed the necessary documentation. Look out for the Tax-Free Shopping logo.

## NIGHTLIFE

Singapore may not have the racy reputation of
Bangkok or Hong Kong, but its nightlife is vibrant
and has changed beyond recognition in the last
few years with much greater variety now on offer.
It is true that in the past its most famous night
sight used to be Bugis Street, where transvestites
promenaded and noisy bars stayed open until
the early hours, but the area disappeared in 1985
when it was bulldozed to make way for the MRT.
However, a sanitized version of Bugis Street has
been re-created, with closed-circuit TV and
plainclothes police to ensure that soliciting does
not occur. Where there are transvestites, these
have been hired as "customer relations officers" to
explain the history of the area to the visiting public.

Today, the visitor can enjoy a wide variety
of experiences from the open-mic evenings at
"Going Om" in Haji Lane to the outdoor movie
screenings at Fort Canning. To gaze upon one of
the best skylines in the world, 1-Altitude in the
city cannot be rivaled. CÉ LA VI and Spago on the
top of Marina Bay Sands are also popular for their
spectacular city views, though visits there come
with a price tag. A cheaper and less touristy version
is Southbridge bar on Boat Quay, which is also
famous for bar hopping, along with Club Street in
Chinatown, where hundreds of people spill onto
the otherwise peaceful Ann Siang Hill on Friday
nights. At the bottom of Club Street you'll find an
army of "party buses" kitted out with disco balls
and strobe lights ready to take you to your next
destination.

Speakeasy-themed bars serving chic and expensive cocktails have popped up across the city, often hidden behind unmarked doors in old Peranakan shophouses. One of the originals is "28 Hong Kong Street" by Clarke Quay MRT. Likewise, the craft beer scene is popular, and if you're up for a drive, you can try out Little Island Brewery for some local flavor.

If pole dancers and tightly packed clubs is your preference, then Bang Bang at the Pan Pacific Hotel merits a visit. If you prefer to dance in your sneakers, try Headquarters on Boat Quay, or Kilo Lounge in Chinatown. Finally, Tanjong Beach Club on Sentosa is an institution, and not just reserved for the night. Generally, nightclubs close around 1:00 a.m. on weekdays and 3:00 a.m. at weekends, although some continue until 6:00 a.m. Note that cover charges and alcohol are expensive, and the dress code is usually smart casual.

The gay clubbing scene is alive and well, and "Tantric" remains its public face. But anyone can go there, and it is filled with locals and foreigners alike. Otherwise, bars come and go. The best place to visit for the latest information is www.utopia-asia.com.

## CULTURE

All the various ethnic groups in Singapore have formed cultural societies to maintain and sustain their identities, and here music and dance play important roles. The playing of the *sitar*, the classical Indian stringed instrument, the staging of colorful operas from Canton, Hokkien, and Teochew, and the magical sound of the Malay *gamelan*, a native version of the Indonesian ensemble of gong and chimes, all contribute to a vibrant cultural life. Every June there is month-long Festival of Arts. In addition, there is an annual film festival and regular productions of live theater.

Furthermore, because of Singapore's colonial background Western ballet and classical music have a large local following, and the city is a regular stopping-off point for performing arts companies touring East and Southeast Asia. "Shakespeare in the Park" is held in May and is a fascinating local interpretation of the various works. It is easy to dip your toe into the varied waters of Singapore's cultural life and the best place to start is the SISTIC Web site, the country's leading provider of event tickets.

Well worth visiting are the Singapore Art Museum, particularly for its outstanding collection of contemporary Asian art, the National Gallery, the National Museum, the Asian Civilisation Museum, and the Esplanade, the huge arts complex on the waterfront east of the Padang, home to the Theatres on the Bay. This bold project reflects the government's drive to foster a unified Singaporean culture.

# chapter seven

# TRAVEL, HEALTH, & SAFETY

## GETTING AROUND

Transportation in and around Singapore, whether by taxi, bus, or Mass Rapid Transit (MRT), is easy and relatively cheap. A good way to see the sights is to take a Hop-on Hop-off bus or enjoy a guided cruise of the Singapore River.

## MRT

The MRT is one of the most efficient underground rail networks in the world. Trains run every day from 5:30 a.m. until midnight. They are clean, air-

conditioned, and outside the city center the track runs overground. You can purchase the contactless Ez-link card at any MRT station for a S $5 non-refundable charge plus S $10 consumable amount (US $4 and $7 respectively in 2018). It is cheaper than cash, but if you intend to spend only a few days in the city it is probably more economical to buy a Singapore Tourist Pass, which has the advantages of lasting two to three days and has a S $10 refundable deposit.

There is also the Changi Airport Skytrain and the Sentosa Express Monorail, which offers transit to Sentosa island from Singapore's mainland.

### Buses and Trams

The bus network is comprehensive and slightly cheaper than the MRT. The Ez-link or Tourist Pass are valid here too, but you must remember to tap in and out. Buses are air-conditioned and operate daily from 6:00 a.m. until midnight. Hop-on Hop-off tourist buses and the amphibious DUCKtours—as well as

TOPless and HiPPO—will take you for a historical spin about the city, while bumboat river cruises down the Singapore River have been running since 1987.

## Taxis

Taxis are plentiful and you can hail them or pick them up at designated stands. You can also download apps for companies such as Comfort and Citycab. Fares are reasonable, and every taxi has them clearly displayed. All cabs are metered and tipping is not expected. Remember though that if you are traveling in the city center—known as the Restricted Zone—you will have to pay a congestion charge; there is a surcharge at peak period times and also after midnight.

Singaporean taxi drivers speak good English and are generally happy to chat, but avoid politics as a topic and remember that a Muslim driver may refuse to take you if you have a dog.

## Trains

Regular train services run between Singapore and key cities and towns on the west coast of Malaysia. Rail travel is safe, comfortable, and relatively cheap and you can go as far as Bangkok in under 48 hours. However, you must purchase a ticket on the shuttle train from Woodlands to Johor Bahru Sentral first. From there, you can take the train of your choice. Remember, you will have to clear Singapore Immigration and Malaysian Customs and Immigration at Woodlands Train Checkpoint.

For a truly luxurious trip, try the Eastern and Oriental Express. It, too, departs from Woodlands Railway Station and takes in the sights of Penang and the River Kwai.

### Rickshaws

You can also hire a rickshaw, or "trishaw" as it is known locally. This is a three-wheeled bicycle with a carriage on the back. Today these are only a tourist attraction, not a regular form of transportation. Remember to negotiate the price before you commence your journey.

### Car Rental

There is no negotiating the cost of renting a car. Rentals are high, parking is expensive, and the government has introduced disincentives to combat traffic congestion. The only benefit of a car is to continue your trip into Malaysia.

For short-term visits, a valid driver's license from your own country or an IDP (International Driving Permit) is required for driving in Singapore.

Driving is on the left and, of course, if you drive into the Restricted Zone in the center of the city there is a charge to pay. The speed limit is 30 miles (50 km) an hour, and 50 miles (80 km) on an expressway. Driving under the influence of drugs or alcohol is dealt with severely.

### WHERE TO STAY

Accommodation options range from luxury to budget. Singapore has some of Asia's most iconic five-star

hotels and also clean hostels for the backpacker. Homestays are possible, and Airbnb is permitted within strict guidelines: a private home can be legally let for a stay of over three-months, and public housing for a stay of over six-months.

A good place to start looking for a hotel is www.stayinsingapore.com, managed by the Singapore Hotel Association.

## HEALTH

Medical care in Singapore is of the highest quality. For this reason, it is wise to carry health insurance as the costs will be high. Singapore spends 4.7 percent of its GDP on health. In 2017 Bloomberg ranked its healthcare system second in the world for efficiency, and it has been held up by many Western countries as a model to replicate. It offers both private and public options, and the type of healthcare a person has access to depends on their immigration status. Citizens and permanent residents are entitled to subsidized government healthcare (of up to 80 percent), which is paid for through the compulsory medical savings program, Medisave (part of an individual's CPF payments, see earlier). Foreigners holding work permits are either covered by their employer or purchase their own private insurance.

There are six clusters of public healthcare facilities as well as the National University Hospital and the Singapore General Hospital. There are four major private hospitals and four major private medical centers. The difference in cost between public and private facilities is negligible, but as private facilities usually have minimal waiting times, expatriates and medical tourists tend to use these more.

If you dial 995 for an ambulance, it will arrive promptly and take you to the nearest hospital for treatment. Otherwise, you do not need an appointment for A&E (accident and emergency) and you can admit yourself. Bear in mind that waiting times can exceed two hours, however.

For non-emergency help, it is best to visit a GP (general practitioner), who can be found in most neighborhoods. They will normally see you without an appointment and can prescribe drugs on the spot.

### Chinese Medicine

Traditional Chinese medicine (TCM) has been practiced for over five thousand years. It aims to heal the body by balancing the functioning of the *yin* and *yang* energies and allowing the *qi* (life energy) to flow freely through the body's meridian points. Its most common practices are acupuncture, cupping therapies, and herbal medicine. TCM practitioners are popular in Singapore, and Singaporean Chinese (as well as many ex-pats) will happily use both TCM and conventional forms medicine.

The sector is highly regulated and clinics are required to register with the Traditional Chinese Medicine Practitioners Board (TCMPB), so check that any practitioner you visit is registered.

## Potential Hazards

The need for inoculations is being debated. Some people consider Singapore safe enough to travel to without any. However, the World Health Organization advises you have the following: hepatitis A and B, typhoid, cholera, yellow fever, Japanese encephalitis, rabies, meningitis, polio, measles, mumps and rubella, Tdap (tetanus, diphtheria, and pertussis), chickenpox, shingles, pneumonia, and influenza. Talk to your local healthcare provider for further advice.

Mosquito-borne illness such as dengue fever and chikungunya virus exist, and it is wise to use mosquito-repellent creams or sprays. You can purchase these easily but look out for the Guardian or Watson pharmacy chains, which are the most popular.

If you suffer from respiratory problems, bear in mind that pollution levels from June to October are high owing to the land-clearing fires in Indonesia.

The Singapore government monitors these levels and you can get updates online at www.haze.gov.sg.

Some prescribed medicines are not available in Singapore and many over-the-counter medications require a prescription. To avoid problems, ensure that you have enough to cover your stay. Otherwise, the Guardian and the Watson chains have a pharmacy that will sell you prescription medicine with a valid doctor's prescription.

---

### EMERGENCY NUMBERS
All numbers are manned by English-speaking staff.

**Ambulance**  995 emergency

1777 non-emergency

**Police**  999

**Fire**  995

---

## RULES AND REGULATIONS
### Fines
Singapore has been dubbed "Fine City." Smoking is not permitted in any public space, including museums, libraries, elevators, theaters, cinemas, air-conditioned restaurants, hair salons, supermarkets, department stores, and government offices. There are tough fines for offenders.

No smoking — Fine $1000

No eating or drinking — Fine $500

No flammable goods — Fine $5000

No durians

Other civil offenses that incur fines include spitting, jaywalking, littering, urinating in an elevator, not flushing a public toilet, chewing gum, walking nude without the curtains drawn, and drinking alcohol in a public place between 10:30 p.m. and 7:00 a.m. Be aware that you cannot purchase e-cigarettes, e-pipes, or e-cigars (or their refills) in the country.

## Drugs
Trafficking in all but the smallest quantity of narcotics is punishable by death. Generally a foreign miscreant is deported on conviction, but this cannot be relied upon. (See below)

## Homosexuality
Male homosexuality is illegal; however the government does not proactively enforce the law. Openly gay social venues do exist, and some can be found in Chinatown.

## Jehovah's Witnesses
Public and private meetings are illegal, and it is against the law to possess any of their publications, including the Jehovah's Witness bible.

## SAFETY
Singapore's reputation as a safe and secure destination is well known, and it enjoys one of the lowest crime rates in the world. Low crime doesn't mean "no crime," however, but any gang activity tends to stay within the community and you are very unlikely to witness it.

## Police and the Law

The Singaporean Police Force has one mission, "to prevent, deter, and detect crime," and its vision is "to make Singapore the safest place in the world." It has a world-wide reputation for being a non-corrupt, efficient force, and in 2018 the new head of CID (Criminal Investigation Department) was a woman.

Offices are armed, and all are fluent in English. The apparent absence of uniformed police in an area does not mean an absence of the police themselves as many are plainclothes officers. In other words, if you are in a brawl outside a nightclub, the police will be close by. Always smile and be respectful.

Following an arrest, your passport will be retained for the length of the legal process, which can be months rather than weeks. You do not have a "right to silence" and they view uncooperative silence as an indication of guilt. However, you do have the right to legal representation, but this is costly and can leave you tens of thousands of dollars out of pocket. The penalty will reflect the seriousness of the crime. If conviction leads to incarceration, you can expect to be in prison for one to three months. Prison is designed to be tough, with inmates spending twenty-three hours a day in a shared cell.

**Corporal and Capital Punishment**

A common punishment in Singapore is caning. It is reserved for men between the ages of eighteen and fifty who are certified to be in a fit state. The legal limit is twenty-four strokes; however most sentences are between three and six. There are over thirty-five offences punishable by caning, including robbery, causing grievous hurt, vandalism, sexual abuse, and rioting. It is mandatory for rape, drug-trafficking, illegal moneylending, and for foreigners who overstay by more than 90 days.

Capital punishment exists in Singapore and though the number of executions has fallen dramatically since 2010, it is still mandatory for the importing and exporting of drugs, as well as possession of high quantities of drugs, such as 500 grams of cannabis. There are foreign nationals on death-row. Pleas for clemency from governments and the United Nations are not always heeded, and a Ghanaian man was hanged in March 2018 for trafficking methamphetamine.

# BUSINESS
# BRIEFING

### THE ECONOMIC MIRACLE

From earliest times, the island's location has been of trading interest to many. Later, when coupled with free-trade colonialism and an influx of immigrants, its economic growth was ensured.

At independence, however, Singapore was a small territory with no natural resources and a poor, unskilled workforce. Prime Minister Lee Kuan Yew and Finance Minister Goh Keng Swee set out a development strategy that made the state the principal investor in an export-oriented free-market system. Using various tax incentives, the government

expanded the island's manufacturing and industrial base by attracting technologically strong foreign companies. The government controlled industrial financing and development and invested heavily in education. The result in the late 1960s was double-digit GDP growth.

Then, in 1971 Britain withdrew from its military bases. The naval base had contributed 20 percent to the island's GDP, but this initial setback proved a blessing in disguise as it forced Singapore to stand on its own two feet and to seek competitive advantage by converting it into the world's third-largest commercial port.

Government policies to expand trade and industry and attract foreign investment paid off. Singapore rode the 1973 oil crisis with slower but, nonetheless, single-digit growth. Tariff protection for the electrical and electronic sectors was reduced and financial services became a focus for growth. By 1975, Singapore was the world's third-largest oil-refining location and the third-busiest port, and five years later it became Asia's most important financial center after Tokyo and Hong Kong. This is when the government targeted computer technology and electronics as the next phase in Singapore's industrial development.

Singapore weathered the 2008 financial crisis but Temasek Holdings (the government-owned national wealth fund) lost close to S $55 million. The country went into recession. Unemployment rose and, after the PAP returned to power in 2011 with fewer seats than expected, the government cut the flow of foreign workers by two-thirds over three years, as migrant workers were blamed for taking jobs and depressing wages. However, by 2016 economic growth was 1.7 percent and growth in industrial production 1 percent.

Competition from China has spurred the government to seek trade alliances and carry out economic restructuring. Nevertheless, China is its largest trading partner, accounting for 14.5 percent of total Singaporean exports in 2017, compared to the USA, which is fifth and accounts for 6.5 percent.

Singapore's success rests on its willingness to adapt its work and management styles and invest in education, skills, and technology. This has been reinforced by the ease of entry for foreign investment in a corruption-free stable economy. It is a member of the ASEAN Free Trade Zone and has bilateral free-trade arrangements with China, India, South Korea, New Zealand, Japan, and the United States.

## FINANCIAL MANAGEMENT

Initially Singapore tied its currency to the US dollar but by the late 1970s the currency had been floated and all controls on currency exchange abolished.

Singapore's compulsory Central Provident Fund (CPF), founded in 1955, deposits a predetermined portion of a worker's income into a tax-exempt account, which the employer near-matches. The scheme has morphed and improved since inception but, currently, the combined employer/employee contribution is 37 percent of salary for under fifty-fives, a level that is beyond comparison. The Fund, which covers worker retirement and disability, also creates consistent budget surpluses and a national savings rate of nearly 50 percent of GDP.

The main concern of the central bank, the Monetary Authority of Singapore (MAS), is price stability, hence use of the exchange rate and not the interest rate to achieve this end. This is because the exchange rate can be controlled through the bank buying and selling the Singapore dollar. As the central bank seeks to preserve the dollar's purchasing power and protect workers' savings, it tends to cut wages rather than devalue the currency.

Singapore trades in shares, bonds, derivatives, and commodities twenty-four hours a day and so overlaps with the trading hours in both the USA and Europe. The financial institutions range from insurance to investment banking.

Singapore, in common with most of Asia, has experienced rapid social change caused by expanding education, access to information, and the social-media environment, so it is no longer possible to talk about a Singaporean mindset. Some companies have embraced modernity and are filled with egalitarian millennials, and some are hidebound family hierarchical businesses or government bureaucracies. In other words, as anywhere, generalize at your peril. Nonetheless, it is useful to note the older habits that may still carry influences.

## BUILDING RELATIONSHIPS

Modern Singapore can seduce the Western businessperson into thinking they are "at home." However, this could be a mistake. There are cultural differences and norms that should be appreciated to ensure a successful trip.

In most countries, but particularly in Asia, a business relationship is founded on trust and mutual respect, so time is needed to develop it. Hence it is not advisable to plunge into business at the outset of a meeting. Singaporeans, like other Asians, prefer to get to know the person they are dealing with. Take time to demonstrate your honor and integrity and take the trouble to maintain contacts and not just establish them.

It is also important to remember that your business relationships should be nurtured with both direct and indirect contact. A failure to do so will expose your business to attack from competitors.

## INTRODUCTIONS

It is normal on introduction to express your pleasure at the meeting. If business enters into the conversation, the discussion should be modest. Do not talk up your business.

The handshake is the normal business introduction, but it should be soft and linger a while. Do not crush the bones or vigorously shake the arm of the other person! Also, depending on the ethnic mix of the company, you might find a woman unwilling to shake hands with a man, although this is uncommon in most international businesses. When you have known someone for a long time, and are of the same sex, the contact time for handshakes and body contact can be longer than some Westerners are used to. Extended handshakes, shoulder clasping, and even body hugs may not be about you but performed for a wider audience, so try to participate without embarrassment.

Avoid drawing quick conclusions from how a person might act when you first meet them; the etiquette is different and often the opposite of what you would expect in the West.

## SMALL TALK

Good topics of polite conversation are positive things about Singapore, including how successful it is, how you enjoy the food, the beautiful scenery, the fascinating culture, and so on. Always start meetings, even if you know the person, with five minutes of general discussion before plunging into the agenda. To do otherwise is to set the wrong tone for the discussions ahead.

Topics to avoid are sex, religion, politics, or criticisms of the government and Singapore in general.

## HANDS

Within the Chinese community items such as gifts, including *hongbao* money and business cards, are given and accepted with two hands. With Malays and Indians never use the left hand for handling food, money, gifts, shaking hands, giving business cards, or any other transaction. However, most Singaporeans, of any religion or ethnicity, are now completely at ease with whatever approach you take, so long as it is gentle and not ostentatious.

When using your right hand, remember not to point at a person; rather use the whole of the right hand, palm upward, in a gesturing motion. When ordering a taxi, simply turn the palm down, beckoning toward yourself.

## BUSINESS CARDS

The Singapore business environment is hierarchical, and it is important to note a person's position in a company. For this reason, business cards are crucial. When you receive them, one side may be written in English and the other in Chinese. Take a minute or two to study them; not only is this courteous but it tells you the position and authority of the person. Have your card printed in both Chinese and English and take local advice as to the most appropriate title to use. This is necessary to ensure you meet the right people in the company. Even if you are embarrassed at your high-sounding title, it has been recommended for a reason.

When handing out business cards, you should give them to everyone present, using both hands, with the print facing the recipient so that it can be read easily. Never put a card in your back pocket or write on someone's business card. Both actions can give offense to the older generation.

## MEETINGS

It is important to plan your discussions in detail before a business meeting. Not only is punctuality vital, but it is a good idea to arrive fifteen minutes before the scheduled time. Members of a team might come from different ethnic groups, so expect the Chinese to shake hands upon greeting, and some older Muslims and Malays to *salaam* (putting their hands together and giving a slight bow saying "*salaam*," or "peace"). Similarly, Hindus might use the same form saying "*namaste*." Again, however, in most international businesses, Western modes of address are commonplace and expected. Business meetings are usually conducted in English and tea is often served at meetings; it is polite to accept it.

Be patient and allow time for reflection. It is also a good idea to restate your position several times if necessary because polite persistence pays off. Never, of course, demonstrate frustration or lose your temper. A warm, friendly attitude emphasizing common aims will always be more constructive. And remember that "yes" does not necessarily mean "I agree"— it is more like "I hear you." Chinese speakers tend to use an indirect style, hinting rather than telling, and sometimes smile to avoid embarrassment when giving bad news.

Always end your meetings with a summary of what was discussed, what was agreed, and what actions are to be carried out and by whom.

## WOMEN IN BUSINESS

Women are well represented in the professions, commerce, and industry, with many holding senior managerial positions. As we've seen, the World Economic Forum gave Singapore a Gender Parity score in 2017 of 0.70, which compares favorably with the 0.701 of the USA. Western business visitors should always observe Singaporean protocols where dress, behavior in the office, and body language are concerned; any sign of flirting could destroy the woman's position and certainly ruin a business deal. Singaporean women tend to dress conservatively and knee-length skirts are the norm.

## SAVING FACE

"Saving face" applies to all three ethnic groups and—as with everything in Singapore—it is not just about individuals but about the group to which they belong. Losing face undermines a person's integrity and moral character. More than that, it undermines the whole group. Most importantly, saving face preserves harmony, whether the group at the time is the family, one's work colleagues, or the nation itself. To embarrass somebody or make them lose face is the most serious mistake you can make as a visitor. They will regard you as shallow and lacking in personal integrity, and someone not to be trusted.

Be careful then about criticism and strong disagreement. If it is essential to be critical, then do so with tact. When disagreeing with someone, try to nudge them gently in the other direction. Never think that you are being too subtle. A Singaporean will always get the hint and respect you for your cultural sensitivities.

Never rebuke a senior in front of a junior, or ask a junior's opinion in front of a senior, or openly praise just one member of the group without including the group as a whole. Within the group they will know who deserves the praise.

Losing one's temper is also seen as a "loss of face," as is any display of strong emotion—a person who is out of control or reveals their emotions too easily cannot be trusted.

## NEGOTIATING STYLES

Successful outcomes with a partner, customer, or supplier are more likely and certainly easier if you appreciate how the person is thinking about the business opportunity or the problem to be solved. Singaporeans do not only think in terms of cause and effect, but also in terms of their intricate network of relationships and the thought patterns that go with them. The Westerner often enjoys talking about the problem and then the solutions. The Singaporean wants to know both the benefits and the impact on relationships within his or her organization.

A focus on the benefits and common ground of any deal or arrangement cannot be stressed too highly. Where there are problems, the Singaporean is prepared to share the burden and will expect this to cut both ways, irrespective of any contractual terms. If there are other existing relationships that will be disadvantaged by the deal, it is well to look for ways of mitigation to ease the mind of the person you are negotiating with. This might mean the arrangements are not as clean-cut as you would like, but it is more likely that the deal will fly.

Your weaknesses will be exploited in attempts to reach a decision—disclose them at your peril. Know your walking away point, hold to this, and do not make early concessions. Stress the package nature of any concession you offer—there must be something in return. Refer to the pressure you are having from the head office or senior management if you are having difficulty in closing a deal.

There are enormous benefits in having a Singaporean on your team. Not only will they pick up shades of meaning that have passed you by, but they will also identify in the meeting—or more likely outside—the crucial issues to be resolved to reach a settlement.

## DECISION MAKING

It is important to know who the decision maker is and what their needs are if they are not the person sitting opposite you. Since the Singaporean is committed to both the contract and the relationship, reaching decisions can be slow. However, implementation is fast once everything is agreed upon.

If a decision seems difficult to achieve, be prepared to table and discuss the benefits and disadvantages to your side as well as the other person, and show how the deal is fair if not ideal.

The one comfort in doing business in Singapore is that it is easier than in most Asian countries, and that there are no "commissions" or side payments to be made once a deal is reached.

## CONTRACTS AND FULFILLMENT

Singaore has been built on the rule of law and solid institutions and as a consequence holds contract law in higher esteem than other countries in the region. When drawing up a contract it is advisable to use a licensed local lawyer. Both sides expect contracts to be honored and fulfilled. However, owing to the nature of business in Asia, a problem is expected to be shared in the event of difficulties, such as escalating raw material costs or a decline in demand. Cooperation and flexibility require you not to follow the small print of the contract to the letter. Arbitration is increasingly used as a way of resolving disputes as people gain confidence in this cheaper and faster alternative to the courts.

## TEAM BUILDING

As Singapore is a "collectivist" culture, teamwork and cooperation are highly valued. Although the younger generation exhibit more individualistic traits, it is true to say that Singaporeans prefer shared responsibility and shared rewards, rather than aggressive individualism and self-promotion. Showing yourself to be innovative and progressive is not conducive to good group dynamics.

Professionalism is important, and in teamwork the leader makes the decisions after lengthy consultations to ensure everyone is on board. Obedience is implicit and it would be bad form for a member of the team to complain about the decision. Because harmony is all-important, working practice tends to be slow and methodical, which can sometimes frustrate foreign managers used to more rapid decision-making. Even so, they appreciate the wisdom of taking the time to reach a decision that is fully supported.

The team leader is responsible not only for selecting its members, but for giving clear, concise instructions, emphasizing the collective nature of the enterprise, making certain that everyone is occupied, and regularly monitoring progress. A good leader will be aware that a smile does not equal satisfaction, and perhaps more importantly that a statement of agreement does not necessarily mean that a person understands. It is essential to give face to everyone and not to criticize a senior in front of the whole team. Only ever comment on poor performance in private. A diligent manager will give encouragement and praise where it is due, but will remember to praise the whole team and not a single individual.

# chapter nine

# COMMUNICATING

## LANGUAGES

In 1965 great consideration was given to the
question of which language should be considered
official in the new polyglot nation. With three
distinctive ethnic groups, it was a highly sensitive
issue, especially as racial tensions often threatened
to explode over minor matters, and, in some cases,
actually did so.

In 1959, when Singapore attained self-
government, it was straightforward: Malay was
declared the official language in order to prepare
the way for entry into the Federation of Malaysia.
All that changed after August 9, 1965, when, thrown
out of the Federation, it had no choice but to earn
its living as an international trading community.
The Singaporean Chinese now actively promoted
Mandarin, their cultural, business, and civic leaders
pointing out to Prime Minister Lee Kuan Yew's
government that it was spoken by more than

新加坡

80 percent of the population. Indeed, in the 1950s all classes of Chinese in Singapore—from businessmen to rickshaw drivers—helped fund a Chinese-language university in Singapore named "Nantah," which became the symbol of their culture and values, language and education.

Lee Kuan Yew, however, had other ideas. The least divisive solution was four official languages: Malay, Mandarin Chinese, Tamil, and English. In this way, no ethnic group had a linguistic advantage.

Malay was to be the language of administration. However, it was not the use of Tamil or Malay that angered the Chinese community but the introduction of English as an official language. They considered this a betrayal, not least because children were forced to learn it at school alongside their own ethnic language. In one leading Chinese newspaper, Lee Kuan Yew and his government were portrayed as "pseudo foreigners who forget their ancestors."

Singapore, however, had a history of excellence as the regional center for education in English, with its schools, arts and science colleges, and teacher-training and medical colleges. The brightest English-educated students from Malaya and Borneo, as well as the former Dutch East Indies (which later became Indonesia), attended these colleges and trained as doctors, teachers, and other professionals as well as administrators. Still, the opposition to English was unremitting. Not until 1978 was Lee Kuan Yew able to persuade Nantah to make English the language of instruction. By then, the majority of Chinese-speaking parents had accepted the change as inevitable, as had the students—finding employment was more difficult for Nantah graduates than those who had been educated in English at the University of Singapore. Although it was a painful adjustment, by the early 1990s Nantah and the University of Singapore felt confident enough to merge and become the National University of Singapore, or NUS as it is now known.

However, the language debate was not over. This time it concerned the status of the different Chinese dialects spoken in Singapore, the predominant ones being Hokkien, Hakka, Hainanese, Hoklo, Hokchiu, and, to a lesser extent, Cantonese (the latter being the dialect spoken in Hong Kong). From the 1980s onward, Lee Kuan Yew encouraged the speaking of Mandarin in the home to help children master it at school. He stopped making speeches in his native Hokkien, and TV and radio program makers were no longer permitted to broadcast in Chinese dialects. To encourage the speaking of the language, he instituted a "speak Mandarin" day once a month.

At first, the insistence on Mandarin was seen by many Singaporean Chinese as an academic exercise: all very well in theory but making no difference to the practical issues of the day. However, the opening up of China, whose official language has always been Mandarin, brought about a swift change of attitude. It soon became clear that those in the workforce, whether professional or technical, could command a premium if they spoke Mandarin as well as English. The handing back of Hong Kong to China in 1997 further underlined the importance of the language. The Beijing government regarded all regional dialects as grossly inferior to it, and Mandarin has always been the language of government and administration, whether Imperial or Communist, and, indeed, for centuries the speaking of Mandarin was the sign of an educated person.

### "Singlish"

The Singaporeans have developed their own way of speaking English, known as "Singlish." This patois is a unique manifestation of Singapore's multiculturalism. It is a mix of different dialects and breaks the rules of English conjunction and grammar, following very much Chinese syntax. So, as one expat explained, you might hear someone saying, "Today damn hot ah. On fan can?" or "How come I ask you call me yesterday, why you no call one?" (See more opposite.)

The government, on the other hand, wants English to be the common bond between all Singaporeans and opposes anything that it sees as "dumbing down" the language. From time to time, it instigates a "speak proper English" campaign. However, in 2015 to mark fifty years of independence, Singlish was recognized as part of the country's culture and heritage.

Even when using the English language, which we know has been taught in Singapore schools for more than fifty years, mistakes and confusion can arise. If you find the way in which something is said upsetting, remember that for most Singaporeans English is not their first language. A phrase that would be perfectly polite in Chinese can sound abrupt and offensive when translated literally into English. For example, in the West we will ask a guest "Would you like a cup of tea?" In Singapore this becomes "You want to drink tea or not?"

Similarly, in Chinese and Malay there are no tense changes; a time phrase is used to indicate past or future. To a foreigner this can sound uneducated when translated directly into English. For example, "I see that movie already with my friend."

The tip here is to be culturally sensitive and not assume that somebody is being rude. Learn to tolerate ambiguity and accept a degree of frustration!

---

### SOME SINGAPOREAN PHRASES

**Kopi** a Malay/Hokkien term for coffee. A coffee-shop is a *kopitiam* (*tiam* being Hokkien for shop).

**Havoc** from the English "disorder," or "confusion," but used here as an adjective: "My son is so havoc he doesn't do his homework and wants to go to clubs!"

**Kayu** from the Malay meaning "stupid": "My son is so kayu, he always gets poor grades at school."

**Lah** a Malay prefix used to emphasize something, as in: "He can do it lah, no problem," or "No lah," meaning "no way."

**Maama** from the Tamil word for uncle, so a "Maama shop" is an Indian/English word meaning a shop run by an Indian merchant.

**Waah!** has no precise meaning, but is an exclamation of excitement and amazement. This word is frequently heard at banquets as each new dish appears.

***Shiok*** from the Malay, expresses approval, happiness, or pleasure, similar to "cool" or "great."

***Can*** a versatile word whose meaning depends much on the tone used. If you want to know if someone can do something, you'll say "can or not?" The answer may be "can lah!" meaning "yes, of course."

***Chop*** refers to the placing of tissue packets on tables in hawker centers to reserve them. Someone might say, "Wah! I chopped the table, lah."

***Blur*** refers to someone who is slow to catch on: "Wah lau! Why you so blur? Everyone knows that, lah."

***Angmoh*** this refers to any Westerner who has fair skin. Once a term of abuse, it is now used without any negative connotation.

***Aiyah*** this usually signifies impatience or dismay.

## BODY LANGUAGE

For Westerners who struggle to conceal anger, frustration, boredom, or tiredness, reading Singaporean body language can be a challenge. Remember that this is a society that values harmony above all else and that avoids causing distress to others. This is why "keeping face" is so important. "Face" is about personal dignity—about having a good name and a good character—and extends to the family, the company, and even the country.

As a consequence, they tend to trust nonverbal messages and tone of voice more than the spoken word, and to allow someone to "save face" they will hint at a point rather than say it directly. Silence is also an important part of communication, as is pausing before answering a question. The Westerner's tendency to reply quickly is seen as thoughtless or rude.

We have seen in the chapter on business that in all three ethnic groups "Yes" does not necessarily mean "I agree." If there is a slight pause, an embarrassed smile, or a sucking through the teeth, the "Yes" probably means "No." The Indian community adds another dimension to the matter of "Yes" and "No." An Indian will wag his head when replying in the affirmative, which a Westerner might mistake for a "No."

In China, you might encounter loud belching after a meal, or spitting in the street, but not nose-blowing. You should be aware that all these actions are considered equally disgusting in Singapore by all groups. If you have a cold and need to blow your nose, you should excuse yourself from the present company and go to the bathroom to do so. You might notice that there are large handkerchiefs for sale in the shops, but these are intended for mopping your brow in the most humid months.

We've seen that pointing with your finger is considered impolite. If you wish to draw a person's attention to something, then use your whole hand or motion with your head. Likewise, be aware of your feet: don't show the soles to others or step over people or their belongings, and do not touch anyone with your foot.

## HUMOR

Humor, especially British humor, does not travel well as it relies heavily on puns, irony, and sarcasm and is often self-deprecating. If a Singaporean asks you, "How many people work hard in your company?" and you reply, "Hardly any," they will conclude the employees are lazy and the company on the verge of bankruptcy. Even if you smile when saying this, they will take this as embarrassment about the poor work ethic in your company. Self-deprecation, in particular, is rarely comprehended, even among the young, who do not readily expose their weaknesses to others in public and would look askance at those who do.

This does not mean the Chinese, Indians, and Malays lack a sense of humor, of course. Theirs tends to be more slapstick, as you will discover if you watch local television and the ever-popular Dim Sum Dollies. Comedy nights are popular, and you can go online to find the latest venues.

## THE MEDIA

The two media groups are SPH (Singapore Press Holdings) and MediaCorp (Media Corporation of Singapore), which publish newspapers and magazines, broadcast on TV, and have comprehensive Web sites and online editions. The Ministry of Information, Communications and the Arts is the government's regulatory body that restricts media content that incites racial or religious hatred or is overly critical of the government. Certain lifestyles are also censored.

## Newspapers and Magazines

Daily newspapers are available in all four official languages, and in English there are the *Straits Times*, the *Business Times*, and the afternoon tabloid the *New Paper*, all owned by SPH, with *Today* being owned by MediaCorp.

The *Straits Times* (and its online version at www.straitstimes.com) is the country's highest-selling newspaper and its oldest, having been established in 1845. It provides broad coverage of local, regional, and international news. The *Business Times* (www.business-times. com.sg) covers commercial and financial issues, while the tabloid *New Paper* (www.tnp.sg) is for local consumption. *Today* (www.todayonline.com) is positioned as a mid-market alternative to the SPH offerings.

All papers are sensitive to the government line on major issues and are not controversial. The international press and magazines are also well represented on the newsstands but will disappear if something offends the country's sensitivities or its government.

Local magazines such as the glossy *Vogue Singapore*, *Singapore Tatler*, *Peak*, *Elle*, and others give an insight into the exclusive side of island life.

## TV and Radio

MediaCorp caters to all four languages and the channels to watch in English are Channel 5 and Channel News Asia, while SPH broadcasts TV in Chinese. Prime 12 offers programs in Malay, Tamil, Japanese, and some European languages, but cable TV is widespread, and American shows are popular.

Turning the FM dial will bring you the MediaCorp stations; these are the most listened to out of the nineteen that exist. Web streams are available, and Class 95.0 remains the most popular of the five English-language stations. There is also Gold 905 with news and music, classical music on Symphony at 92.4, sixteen hours news on 938Now, Class 95, and 987. And the BBC World Service.

## TELECOMMUNICATIONS

There are two telecom companies in Singapore offering the full broadband/multimedia, and e-service range: SingTel (with hubs in Singapore, Indonesia, Thailand, Philippines, India, and Australia), and StarHub, owned by Singapore Technologies (ST) and global players BT and NTT.

The international dialing code for Singapore is 0065. Local calls cost very little and nearly all Singaporeans have cell phones. If you want to use your cell phone while in Singapore, check with your provider as to the cost. Otherwise you can buy a local top-up SIM card from any 7-Eleven, the twenty-four-hour convenience store Cheers, or at the airport; you will need your passport however. The three main providers are SingTel, Starhub, and M1, offering a variety of packages for local and international calls.

## THE INTERNET

Singapore aims to be the world's first "Smart Nation" so connectivity is easy. SingTel, Starhub, and M1 are the three main Internet providers, with SingTel and Starhub being fully fiber-optic. Moreover, free public Wi-Fi is extensive and available in many local spots such as malls, museums, MRT stations, and café chains such as Coffee Bean (although in some places you might have to pay a fixed amount for a faster connection). Purchasing a pocket Wi-Fi could be a good idea if you have multiple devices and do not intend to be calling often. These can be rented from any "Changi Recommends" counter at Changi airport, and are dropped off when you leave the country. For those who are going to spend more than a few days in the country, a useful Web site is www.expatsingapore.com.

## POSTAL SERVICES

Mail is usually delivered by the next working day through a network of fifty-seven post offices around the island. Information about rates and delivery times, as well as other services can be found on Singpost's Web site: www.singpost.com. There is also a mobile app.

Express services and courier companies offer local and international destination services. Their rates vary but the major companies are DHL, Fedex, UPS, OCS, and TNT.

Singpost offers, in addition, distinctive services such as SAMs, or self-service automated machines. These are dotted around the island. Here you can weigh postal items, pay fines and telephone/utility bills, and buy stamps at any time, day or night. Speedpost is also available and is an express service that delivers internally and to more than 220 destinations worldwide.

## CONCLUSION

E. M. Forster famously said that the first person you meet when you go abroad is yourself. Once outside the familiar boundaries of your own culture, your sense of self is challenged, and you can be surprised by how you act and think in unfamiliar situations. This is partly why foreign travel is so exciting. If some of the many dos and don'ts listed here seem a little daunting—relax. The Singaporeans understand that you are a stranger in their land and will not expect you to be familiar with their customs, but they will be delighted if you attempt to learn something about their culture. This guide aims set you on the road toward a fuller appreciation of this uniquely rich and varied society.

# Further Reading

Bracken, Gregory Byrne. *Singapore – a walking tour.* Singapore: Marshall Cavendish, 2009.

Braddon, Russell. *The Naked Island.* Edinburgh: Birlinn Ltd, 2002.

Clavell, James. *King Rat.* New York: Dell, 1986.

George, Cheria. *The Air-conditioned Nation.* Singapore: Landmark Books, 2000.

Keay, John. *The Honourable Company: A History of the English East India Company.* London: HarperCollins, 1991.

Lee Kuan Yew. *From Third World to First: The Singapore Story 1965–2000.* New York: HarperCollins, 2000.

Lewis, Mark. *The Rough Guide to Singapore.* New York: Rough Guides, 2016.

Lim, Suchen Christine. *Fistful of Colours.* Singapore: EPB Publishers, 1993.

Seagrave, Sterling. *Lords of the Rim: The Invisible Empire of the Overseas Chinese.* New York: Putnam Publishing, 2000.

SarDesai, D. R. *Southeast Asia: Past & Present.* Colorado: Westview Press, 2003.

TalkingCock.com. *The Coxford Singlish Dictionary.* Singapore: Angsana Books, 2002.

Tan, Cheryl Lu-Lien. *Singapore Noir.* New York: Akashic Books, 2014.

Tan, Kok Seng. *Son of Singapore: Autobiography of a Coolie.* Singapore: Heinemann Asia, 1989.

Wibisono, Djoko. *The Food of Singapore: Simple Street Recipes from the Lion City.* Singapore: Periplus Editions, 2015

Wise, Michael. *Travellers' Tales of Old Singapore.* Connecticut: Weatherhill, 1996.

culture smart! **singapore**

# Index

accommodations 132–3
address, forms of 88, 90–3
age structure 11
air-conditioning 13, 123
alcohol 80, 89, 99, 103, 108, 126, 137
apartments 33, 34, 35, 84–5
area 10, 12, 41
arrests 138–9
Asian values 42–3
Association of Southeast Asian Nations (ASEAN) 32, 142
ATMs 122
attitudes *see* values and attitudes

ballet 127
banks 122
banquets 95–6, 104–7
bars 125–6
beer 102–3
birth rate 33–4, 36
birthdays 69
births 70–1
Boat Quay 117
boat trips 130
body language 158–9
Botanic Gardens 13, 14, 120
British 23–8
Buddhism 47–9, 52
Budi 55
Bukit Brown 40, 78
Bukit Timah Hill 12, 15
burials 78
buses 129
business briefing 140–51
business cards 146

caning 37, 139
capital punishment 139
car rental 132
cell phones 162
Central Development Fund 35–7
Central Provident Fund (CPF) 35–6, 142
Changi airport 110
Changi jail 29

chewing gum 37, 137
child care 36
children 11, 36, 83–4, 86
Chinatown 110–12
Chinese community 16–19, 33, 42
customs and traditions 69–73, 76–7, 79–80
food and drink 95–7, 98–9, 104–5
languages 152–3, 154–5
names 91–2
religion 44–52
Chinese Garden 120
Chinese medicine 134–5
Chinese New Year 60–96
chopsticks 104–5, 107
Christianity 57–8
Christmas 68
citizenship 21
Clarke Quay 117–18
climate 10, 13
colonial rule 23–8
Commonwealth 31
communications 152–64
Confucianism 49–52
contracts 150
conversation, topics of 86, 87, 145
cooking styles 94–8
corporal punishment 37–8, 139
corruption 31, 32
courtship 89
credit cards 122
cremations 78
crime 137
Crown Colony 30
culture 126–7
currency 10, 122, 142
customs and traditions 60–81
cutlery 104–5
*cze chas* (eating houses) 102

dating 89
decision making 150

Deepavali (Diwali) 43, 66–7
Dempsey Hill 118–19
department stores 119, 123
dietary restrictions 98–9, 103, 108
dogs 54, 81, 89, 130
domestic workers 21
Dragon Boat Festival 63–4
dress code 85–6, 126
drinks 102–3
drugs 137, 139
Dutch 23
duty 57

East India Company 23, 25
eating out 104–9
economic miracle 140–2
economy 11, 32
education 33, 36, 59, 83
Eid al-Fitr 67–8
elections 39
electricity 11
emergency numbers 136
English language 16, 36, 83–4, 153–4
entertaining 104–9
environmental issues 41
equality of opportunity 32, 42
equilibrium 45
ethnic makeup 8, 10, 15–21, 37
etiquette 85–6, 159
eating 104–5
food courts 101
hands 145
introductions 144–5
expat community 21
extended family 82

family 11, 42, 82
Family Planning and Population Board 34
Federation of Malaysia 8, 31, 152
feet 86, 159
Feng Shui 79
festivals 60–9

financial management 142–3
fines 37, 136–7
First World War 28
Five Pillars of Islam 53
flora and fauna 13–15
flowers 79–80, 81
food 94–102
food courts 100–1
foreign investment 141, 142
Fort Canning 29, 69, 116, 125
funerals 76–8

Gardens by the Bay 14, 117, 120
gay scene 126, 137
GDP 11, 110, 133, 141, 142
gender equality 36, 82, 147
geography 12–13
gift giving 78–81, 85
goal-oriented approach 59
Goh Keng Swee 140
Goods and Services Tax (GST) 123, 124
government 10
greetings 87–8, 146

hands 145
handshakes 86, 87, 88, 144, 146
Hari Raya Puasa 67–8
harmony 44, 46, 49, 55, 79, 158
health 133–6
health care 33, 35, 133–4
hierarchy 42, 51, 143
Hinduism 52, 56–7
history 22–32
holidays 60–9
home, invitations 85–7
home life 82–93
home ownership 36, 39
homestays 133
homosexuality 126, 137
*hongbao/angbao* (red pockets) 62, 63, 72, 73, 80,m145
hospitals 134

hotels 132–3
housing 84–5
Housing Development Board (HDB) 33, 34–5, 37, 40
humor 87, 160
Hungry Ghosts Festival 64–5

immigration 15–16, 21, 140
independence 30–2
Indian community 20–1, 33, 42
  customs and traditions 71, 75–6, 78, 81
  food and drink 98, 99, 104
  names 93
  religion 55–8
indirect approach 43, 147, 159
Indonesia 122
industry 141
inoculations 135
Internet 11, 162–3
introductions 90, 144–5
invitations
  home 85–7
  reciprocating 107–9
Islam 44, 52–5, 77

Japanese expats 30
Japanese occupation 28–30, 116
jaywalking 37, 137
Jehovah's Witnesses 137
Johore, Sultanate of 22, 24
Joo Chiat (Katong) 118
judiciary 38

Kampong Glam (Arab Street) 113–14
*kampongs* (villages) 34–5, 121
*kiasu* (status anxiety) 8, 59
*kopitams* (coffee shops) 101
Kranji War Memorial 29
Kusu Island 121

labor market 33

land ownership 40
land reclamation 40–1
languages 10, 16, 152–8
Lantern Festival 65–6
law and order 37–8
Lee Hsien Loong 33
Lee Kuan Yew 8, 19, 31, 32–3, 39, 58, 84, 140, 152, 153, 154
left hand 86, 104, 145
leisure time 110–27
life expectancy 11
lifestyle 84–5
Lim Bo Seng 29
literacy 11, 33
Little India 114–15
loss of face 42, 148, 158–9
lunar calendar, Chinese 69

MacRitchie Reservoir 15
Malay community 19–20, 33, 42
  customs and traditions 70–1, 73–5, 77, 80–1
  food and drink 97, 99, 104, 105
  names 92–3
  religion 52–5
Malay language 16, 19, 31, 153
Malaysia Agreement 31
malls 123
Mandarin 16, 17, 83, 152–3, 154–5
Marina Bay 41, 116–17
marriage 89
media 11, 160–2
meetings 146–7
Merlion 22
migrant community 21
money 122
monsoon 10, 13
mosques 54–5, 114
mosquitoes 135
MRT 128–9
multiculturalism 8, 31, 33, 37, 39
museums and galleries 127
music 126–7

culture smart! **singapore**

names 90–3
National Day 31, 43, 65
national identity 8, 31
National Orchid
    Garden 14
nationalism 30
negotiating styles 148–9
New Year's Eve 69
newspapers and
    magazines 161
nightlife 125–6
nudity 37, 137

obligation 49, 50–1, 57
Orchard 119
Orchard Road 123

Padang 116
paternalism 51–2
paternity leave 36
patriarchal society 82
people 15–21
People's Action Party
    (PAP) 31, 32, 33,
    38–9, 141
Peranakan cuisine
    96–7
Peranakans see Straits
    Chinese
pharmacies 135, 136
police 38, 138
politics 38–40
pollution 135–6
Polo, Marco 22, 52
population 10, 12, 21
postal services 163–4
press freedom 39
public displays of
    affection 83, 86, 88
public holidays 43, 60
public and private areas
    86–7
public toilets 37, 137
Pulau Ubin 35, 121–2

radio 162
Raffles Hotel 103, 118
Raffles, Sir Stamford
    23–6, 110, 113, 116,
    121
rainfall 13
Ramadan 54
recession 141
reincarnation 57
relationship-based
    dealings 42–3, 59,
    143–4

religion 10, 43–58
restaurants 95–102,
    104–9
rickshaws 131
Robertson Quay 118
rules and regulations
    136–7, 137

safety 137–9
St. John's Island 121
sales 124
schools 59, 83
seating arrangements
    106–7, 108
Second World War
    28–30
secular state 43
Sentosa 120–1
service charge 123
sex, attitudes toward
    89, 90
shoes, removal of 85
shophouses 111–12,
    117, 126
shopping 119, 123–4
Sikhs 55, 93
Singapore City 12–13
Singapore River 117,
    130
Singapore Sling 103
Singlish 155–8
small talk 145
smoking 37, 136, 137
social change 33–7, 143
social security 33, 35
speeches 107
spitting 37, 137
Sri Mariamman
    Temple 112
standard of living 39
status 42, 51, 59
Straits Chinese 18–19
Straits Settlements
    26–7, 30
Suez Canal 27
Sun Yat Sen 18–19
Sungei Buloh Wetland
    Reserve 15
Supertrees 14, 117
Sustainable Singapore
    Blueprint 41

taboos 54, 81, 82,
    86, 89
    dietary
    restrictions 98–9,
    103, 108

Tamil language 16,
    31, 153
Taoism 44–7
taxes 124
taxis 130
tea 102, 147
team building 151
telephone services
    11, 162
television 161
temperatures 13
Temple of the Tooth
    112
Theatres on the Bay
    127
Thian Hock Keng
    46–7, 116
time, attitudes toward
    43
time zone 11
Tiong Bahru 118
tipping 123
toasts 107
tourism 110
trade 23–4, 26, 31, 140,
    141, 142
trains 130–1
transportation 128–32

United Nations 31
urban development
    40–1
Urban Redevelopment
    Authority (URA) 40

values and attitudes
    42–59
vandalism 37
Vesak Day 63

weddings 71–6
Western cuisine 98
women
    in business 147
    and opposite sex 86,
    87, 88, 89–90, 144
    position of 36, 82
Workers' Party 39

Yin and Yang 45, 46,
    69, 70, 134
young people 52, 59